SUSAN O'BRIEN'S culinary skills developed from three critical factors: her long-standing interest in nutrition and natural foods; her own special dietary needs; and her desire to provide her sons with nutritional homemade meals. She is a gourmet cook, baker, cooking instructor, food management consultant, guest speaker, and the owner of two businesses, O'Brien's Kitchen and O'Brien's Consulting. Susan is also co-author of *CME Consult*, a bimonthly article published by *Medical Meetings Magazine*. She has two grown sons and lives in Gig Harbor, Washington.

Gluten-free, Sugar-free Cooking

Susan O'Brien

Gluten-free, Sugar-free
Cooking

**Over 200 Delicious Recipes to Help You
Live a Healthier, Allergy-Free Life**

Da Capo
LIFE
LONG

A Member of the Perseus Books Group

Copyright © 2006 by Susan O'Brien
Foreword © 2006 by Robert H. Lerman
Introduction © 2006 by Barb Schlitz

Designed by Pauline Neuwirth, Neuwirth & Associates, Inc.
Set in 11 point Baskerville MT by the Perseus Books Group

Cataloging-in-Publication data for this book is available from the Library of Congress.

ISBN: 978-1-56924-293-3

Published by Da Capo Press
A Member of the Perseus Books Group
www.dacapopress.com
Note: The information in this book is true and complete to the best of our knowledge. This book is intended only as an informative guide for those wishing to know more about health issues. In no way is this book intended to replace, countermand, or conflict with the advice given to you by your own physician. The ultimate decision concerning care should be made between you and your doctor. We strongly recommend you follow his or her advice. Information in this book is general and is offered with no guarantees on the part of the authors or Da Capo Press. The authors and publisher disclaim all liability in connection with the use of this book. The names and identifying details of people associated with events described in this book have been changed. Any similarity to actual persons is coincidental.

Da Capo Press books are available at special discounts for bulk purchases in the U.S. by corporations, institutions, and other organizations. For more information, please contact the Special Markets Department at the Perseus Books Group, 2300 Chestnut Street, Suite 200, Philadelphia, PA, 19103, or call (800) 255-1514, or e-mail special.markets@perseusbooks.com.

This book is dedicated to my mother,
Dorothy Kezich O'Brien

Contents

Foreword

Seven and a half years ago, after more than twenty years at a major medical center in Boston, I moved to Gig Harbor, Washington, to begin work at the Functional Medicine Research Center (FMRC). There I had the great pleasure of meeting and working closely with Sue O'Brien, and also of tasting some of her wonderful recipes.

My work at the FMRC was devoted to clinical research in the emerging field of Functional Medicine, a patient-centered, science-based health-care approach that assesses and treats underlying causes of illness through individually tailored therapies. One of the missions of our research effort was to develop case histories for teaching purposes. Thus I began managing patients with complex medical conditions.

Sue volunteered to be one of my first study subjects as I began my research in the FMRC. Sue's medical problems were confusing and challenging, but we patiently worked together to determine the underlying causes of her medical symptoms. Evaluation included an Elimination Diet that required her to stop eating most of her favorite foods. Using this approach we discovered that many of her symptoms disappeared, only to recur when she ate wheat, dairy, and several other foods. In short, she had been suffering from a variety of food hypersensitivities and intolerances. Treatment, unfortunately, required that Sue severely restrict her diet for several months.

Rather than face eating monotonous and depressing meals and snacks, Sue took the dietary change as a challenge. She transformed old recipes into new, and invented others, incorporating allowed ingredients and totally eliminating those that she needed to avoid.

She quickly realized that many others could benefit from her discoveries. She prepared many wheat-free, gluten-free, dairy-free, sugar-free snacks for a course for health professionals on Functional Medicine that we continue to run two to three times a year.

At each session of the course, she would be repeatedly asked by medical doctors, chiropractors, naturopaths, and other health professionals: "Please write a book with these recipes!"

Well, *Gluten-free, Sugar-free Cooking* is that book, and it promises to provide a wonderful selection for those who suffer, as Sue had, with food sensitivities or food intolerances, and for those who would just like a more healthful snack or meal. Sue's health is much improved thanks to these recipes, which help her avoid her problem foods.

Now, it's your turn to benefit from Sue's expertise. Happy reading, happy eating, and good health!

ROBERT H. LERMAN, MD, PhD

Director of Medical Education
The Institute for Functional Medicine
Gig Harbor, WA

Medical Director
Functional Medicine Research Center
Metagenics, Inc.
Gig Harbor, WA

Preface

SEVERAL YEARS AGO, I became employed at the Institute for Functional Medicine, a division of the company that owned the Functional Medicine Research Center in Gig Harbor, WA. The research center was conducting a study, and I applied to participate. I have always been interested in improving my health, and had for years struggled with digestive problems, so I hoped this study might help me get to the root of the problem. The first step in determining my eligibility for the study included completing comprehensive medical questionnaires. The next step was to complete a set of lab tests. I did not qualify for that particular study, but the results of my lab work showed I had several underlying problems, and I became a patient of the clinic.

The first step once I became a patient was to participate in an Elimination Diet, a very useful tool proven to determine whether a person has food allergies. Because there are many foods that commonly cause allergic reactions, (e.g. peanuts, wheat, corn, dairy, etc.) the Elimination Diet removes the most common allergenic foods from your diet for a specific period of time. When the food is reintroduced into the body, you will either have a noticeable reaction to it or not. To determine which food you are reacting to, it is necessary to add just one food back at a time, and wait for a period of four days before adding another.

I carefully complied with the Elimination Diet, as I was very determined to get to the root of my digestive problems. I couldn't wait to begin adding foods back into my diet, and the first food I added back was wheat. I had a dinner that included wheat tortillas that first evening. Within an hour I had a terrible headache; although I didn't connect it with a food reaction. I still had the headache the following morning, along with a rash on both of my legs. I waited four days and then ate wheat again (I didn't want to believe I actually had a food allergy—especially to wheat!). The same thing happened. Slowly, I began the process of adding other foods back into my diet, watching for reactions, and keeping a journal of them, which I then discussed with my health-care practitioner.

Once I had accepted the fact that I had a sensitivity to wheat/gluten, I began the arduous process of finding foods to replace my old favorites. That is how my first book, *Wheat-free, Sugar-free Gourmet Cooking*, came into being. I was determined to find foods that not only were easy to make, but also tasted good. I wanted to be able to enjoy the foods I ate, and I knew that would take some work. I set about going through all my old favorite recipes and experimented with them to make them wheat/gluten and sugar free.

I was fortunate that I worked for an organization at that time that conducted medical conferences based on nutrition for health-care professionals. The practitioners who attended these conferences came from all over the world and had one thing in common. They believed nutrition was the foundation for good health. So, the meals and refreshments we served were made from my recipes of wheat/gluten-free, sugar-free dishes and desserts. The outcome? They loved them! They begged me for the recipes, for themselves and their patients. They applauded my efforts and encouraged me to write a cookbook.

It is my sincere hope that *Gluten-free, Sugar-free Cooking* will offer you a new way of eating and a new way of thinking about cooking without gluten and refined sugars. All it takes is a commitment to your health, creativity in the kitchen, and a good sense of humor!

This book is not limited to individuals who want to eliminate sugar or gluten from their diets because of an illness or allergy. This book is for anyone who wants to live well without refined sugars and gluten. It is amazing how good the recipes are, how easy they are to make.

I hope this cookbook inspires you to be creative and to live your best, most healthful life.

Susan O'Brien

introduction

Each day, more people become aware of the connection between the way they feel and the food they eat. Do you suffer from chronic joint and muscle pain, gastric upset, insomnia, headaches, or fatigue? As we grow older, the list of chronic complaints grows longer. My patients are often astonished when they discover that removal of a particular food causes their joint pain to improve, headaches to decrease, plus they sleep better and have an increase in energy.

Are you trying to avoid wheat, refined sugars, and/or dairy products? What do you eat instead? These foods are common ones that are poorly tolerated by millions of Americans, probably because we overeat wheat, sugar, and dairy many times a day. I felt very deprived and quite irritated when I first realized that these foods were causing my headaches, fatigue, and joint and muscle pain. I struggled to modify recipes that would be easy to prepare and also taste good. At first it felt like I would never be able to eat a yummy dessert again!

Sue O'Brien has made this task easy for those of us looking for good-tasting, gluten-free, sugar-free, and usually dairy-free recipes. Even if you are merely trying to improve the quality of your diet, this is the cookbook for you. Sue has used healthy alternatives to refined sugar and has tried recipes repeatedly to find just the right combination and types of sweeteners and flours. She, herself, has been faced with many food allergies and is aware of the plight facing many of you as you try to find good-tasting alternatives to many of the recipes you were using on a daily basis. She has tried many substitutions for the usual sugar and gluten in recipes and has been begged by her colleagues to SHARE her final results!

It is hard to believe these recipes contain no refined sugar, proof that eating healthfully can still be delicious. Sue's recipes have been developed for those who cannot tolerate refined sugars such as corn syrup, brown sugar, sucrose, dextrose, and also honey. She has developed many of these recipes using a fruit sweetener, which is quite easy to use and is found in most health food stores. And these recipes look as good as they taste!

Good-tasting, sugar-free and gluten-free recipes are so important to those with food allergies and their families. I highly recommend these to my patients, and not only to anyone with food allergies or diabetes, but also to those who are health-conscious and are looking to use less refined sweeteners and better-quality grains in their diet. I have been practicing as a Nutrition Consultant for nineteen years and this is the first cookbook I've seen that combines good, nutritious ingredients with the wonderful taste of "real" food.

Bon appétit.

Barb Schiltz, RN, MS

Nutrition Consultant
Functional Medicine Research Center
Gig Harbor, WA

Sugar and Sugar Alternatives

SUGAR USUALLY COMES from cane, and cane is a form of grass, which is related to wheat. Wheat is a very common allergen, so those with allergies to wheat should consider alternatives to refined cane sugar. Some sugars do come from other sources, such as beets, which are a tuber. When you buy sugar in the grocery store, it is typically cane sugar. You can search the health food stores for beet sugar, but either way, refined sugar is full of empty calories, and has no nutritional value.

Individuals who have allergies to wheat are better off using cactus nectar, fruit sweeteners, blackstrap molasses, or maple syrup as a replacement for sugar. If you have diabetes or problems with yeast conditions, such as candida, you will want to avoid all forms of sugar. If you can tolerate small amounts of sweetness, you may want to try the following substitutions.

■ Fruit Sweeteners

Fruit sweeteners are made from a combination of fruit that has been pressed into juice, creating a concentrated liquid that is then reduced for a long time. Its consistency is slightly thinner than honey. The flavor is quite good. The combination that I use most is the peach, pear, and pineapple combination. You can also find it in apple, white and red grape, and raspberry. It can be found in the refrigerator section of most natural foods stores. You must keep them refrigerated, but use them at room temperature for best results. In the United States, the two brands that I use are Mystic Lake Dairy and Wax Orchards. The Wax Orchards brand does not require refrigeration. Check with your health food stores for the brands available in your geographical area. These sweeteners are better then refined sugar, but still higher in natural sugar then some of the other options

When making the shift to a fruit sweetener from sugar, remember that you are going to cut the amount of sugar by up to half in all of your recipes, depending on the substitution you have chosen. If your current recipe calls for 1 cup of sugar, you would use ½ cup of fruit sweetener. If the product has an aftertaste, reduce the amount of fruit sweetener slightly in the future. Check the labels on the jar for exact conversions.

If you are creaming butter and a sweetener together, be sure they are both at the same temperature or they will not blend well. Cream them long enough for them to become light and fluffy. Again, if the baked product has an acid aftertaste, add baking soda to the recipe to neutralize the acidity of the fruit. Try ½ teaspoon for each 2 cups of batter or dough, or try reducing the amount of sweetener.

Frozen fruit juice concentrates can also be used, as long as they are sugar free. The juice will need to be boiled for about 10 minutes. Reduce the heat, and simmer to thicken. Apple juice works best, and can be found in all grocery stores. Concentrated fruit juice must be kept in the refrigerator or freezer, and will keep for up to two weeks.

■ Amazake

Amazake is a whole-grain product made of water, brown rice, and koji (rice, aspergillus oryzae, and sea salt). The mixture is fermented into a thick liquid. It is high in iron and vitamin B. Plain is best for baking, but it comes in other flavors. It can be found in natural food stores in either the freezer or refrigerator. It can be stored up to one week after it has been opened, and must be kept in the refrigerator. It has a texture similar to honey, and can be used like concentrated fruit sweeteners.

■ Brown Rice Syrup

Brown rice syrup is made from brown rice, water, and 1 percent natural fungal enzymes. Lundberg Farms is a common brand name that can be found in almost every health food store in the United States. It is made in Richvale, California. If you cannot find it in your local market, you can contact Lundberg Farms at www.lundberg.com. You can also call them at 530-882-4551. The product is made using entirely natural processing. This process converts the starches to natural sugars called *maltose*. The liquid is cooked until it thickens. It is very easy to bake with. I use it in my granola bars. It is sticky, and holds them together well. It can be used in recipes in place of honey, molasses, or other syrups. I do not use this in muffins or cakes, as it is so dense it does that not always cook all the way through.

■ Agave Cactus Nectar

I really love this sweetener! It comes from the pineapple-shaped core of the agave, a cactuslike plant native to Mexico. This sweetener is low on the glycemic index (scoring 11 out of 100), has no aftertaste, and is 25 percent sweeter than sugar. It comes in two varieties. The dark version contains more minerals, calcium, iron, potassium, and magnesium. The lighter version is filtered, and has a lighter taste. One teaspoon of the cactus nectar contains about 20 calories, 0 grams of fat, 5 grams of carbohydrates, 5 grams of sugar, 5 grams of sodium, and 0 grams of protein. Sweet Cactus Farms is the brand I prefer. They can be contacted by e-mail at the address agave@sweetcactusfarms.com. Be sure to cut the amount of sweetener by ¼ cup and reduce the heat by 25 degrees F. I also recommend cutting the liquids in the recipe by one-third.

To purchase agave nectar in bulk, see reference list (page 11). I have listed a few places that provide gallon-size containers of this sweetener. It is worth buying the larger size, as it is cheaper in the long run, and lasts much longer than the smaller bottles sold in the stores.

■ Kiwi Sweetener

Another alternative to sugar, suitable for those with diabetes or hypoglycemia, is a kiwi sweetener. It is made from the natural fruit glycosides, polysaccharides, and ketohexose monosaccharides of the kiwi fruit. It contains 0 fat, 0 calories, and 0 carbohydrates. It is about 15 percent sweeter than sugar, and has no aftertaste. The brand Thermosweet contains no dairy, wheat, gluten, artificial colors, flavors, or animal derivatives. See reference list (page 11).

■ Honey, Molasses, and Maple Syrup

If you want to use honey, remember that it is twice as sweet as sugar, and you will want to decrease the amount in a recipe. I would recommend you cut the amount of honey in half. Honey, maple syrup, and molasses all change the liquid-to-dry proportions in a recipe. It is best to first mix the liquid ingredients (at room temperature) with the oil or nondairy margarine/shortening in baking recipes. I recommend beating these together until they become thick, and then adding the other ingredients as directed. Be sure to have all ingredients at the same temperature, or curdling may occur.

For the most part, I do not use honey, molasses, or maple syrup in my recipes. There are a few recipes that include molasses. Be sure to use organic, unsulphured molasses. If you want to substitute these sweeteners for the fruit sweeteners I have mentioned above, please feel free to experiment.

I believe you can achieve the sweetness you desire without using sugar, honey, maple syrup, and molasses, but you be the judge! This cookbook is designed to be a guide only.

Wheat/Gluten Substitutions

THIS IS A very interesting topic. I have always eaten wheat; in fact, I believed that eating foods made from whole wheat were good for me. Through my own dietary challenges and research, I have found this is simply not true for everyone. There is more awareness in the complementary health care field about wheat/gluten, and the possible harm it may cause for some individuals. This may include individuals who are allergic or intolerant of wheat/gluten and other grains in the grass family. People who have other health issues, such as celiac disease, Crohn's disease, irritable bowel syndrome (IBS), autism, ADD, ADHD, chronic fatigue, and other conditions may also need to avoid gluten. If you want or need to avoid gluten entirely, you will also need to eliminate barley, rye, kamut, and spelt (see page 18 for other foods to avoid).

I must tell you, this was quite a shift for me to make. I resisted giving up wheat, and felt frustrated that I couldn't eat the foods I dearly loved. When I first gave up wheat/gluten, I didn't know what to eat in its place. I was hungry. I was losing weight. I was very frustrated. I began reading all of my old cookbooks, trying to determine which recipes I could convert, and then trying to figure out which flour would be the best replacement. I have found many new flours to experiment with. For example, bean flours, such as garbanzo bean flour, are rich in protein and very flavorful. Bob's Red Mill brand carries many flours and prepackaged mixes that are gluten, wheat, and sugar free.

Listed below are other flours that you can use, and what they are best used for.

■ White Rice Flour

White rice flour is a somewhat grainy, bland flour that is milled from polished white rice. It works best in combination with other flours, such as potato, buckwheat, or corn flour. It can be used in cakes, breads, and cookies. It stores well. (I store mine in the refrigerator to keep it fresh, but it is not required.) There are different textures of white rice flour. The most common texture is fine, but regular is also available in health food stores.

■ BROWN RICE FLOUR

I use this flour for many of my recipes. I like it because it contains more nutrients. It is milled from unpolished brown rice. It has a nutty taste, and I like to use it in muffins and cookies. I also use it for my cobblers and Marionberry Bars. I store this flour in the refrigerator, as it contains more oils and has a shorter shelf life. It is also great combined with other flours such as sorghum, millet, garbanzo bean, or almond meal.

■ BEAN FLOUR

I use garbanzo bean and lentil flours for cookies; they can also be added to other flours (rice, for instance) quite well. They offset the grainy texture of rice flour and give it a nice flavor. These flours make good thickeners as well. I recommend you experiment with them. They do not need to be stored in the refrigerator.

■ BUCKWHEAT FLOUR

Buckwheat flour is a member of the rhubarb family. Its name is very misleading. It is not related to wheat. It is not even a grain. It is rich in iron, vitamin B, and calcium. It has a strong grainy flavor. It is best used in waffles, pancakes, breads, and noodles.

■ QUINOA FLOUR

Quinoa (pronounced "keen-wa") flour is high in protein, containing 20 amino acids, including the 10 "essential amino acids." It also contains vitamins A, C, D, B_1, B_2, E, folic acid, niacin, calcium, iron, and phosphorus. It can be used in cookies, pies, cakes, and pasta. It has a light, pleasant taste, and works well combined with other flours.

■ ALMOND MEAL FLOUR

Almond meal flour is made up of blanched almonds that have been finely ground. It is a great source of protein and is rich in fiber, vitamin E, and magnesium. It adds a rich, buttery flavor to cookies, muffins, cakes, pie crusts, and other desserts. It can also be used for breading. It should be stored in the refrigerator.

■ TAPIOCA FLOUR

Tapioca flour is also called tapioca starch, so if you are searching for it in the store, don't be dismayed if you can't find tapioca flour. I went to two stores before I figured out they were the same thing. I do not use these flours alone, but combine them with other flours. Tapioca mixed with brown or white rice flour and potato flour makes wonderful flour. Do not attempt to make pizza dough out of this combination, though. I did and it bombed!

■ AMARANTH FLOUR

This flour has a strong taste. It is good used in breading, thickening sauces, and baking. Mix 25 percent amaranth flour with other flours, such as brown rice flour, quinoa flour, or oat flour, to make up 100 percent. This flour is high in protein and fiber. It contains amino acids, high levels of lysine, vitamins C, B, calcium, potassium, iron, zinc, and niacin. I store amaranth flour in the refrigerator, as the flour tends to develop a stronger taste as it ages.

■ OAT FLOUR

This flour isn't for everybody. If you react to oats, you will want to avoid oat flour. It's a nice flour, and is good in cookies and muffins. It tends to brown, so use it with caution for sauces. It is too heavy to use for cakes, but does make nice cookies. This can be stored in a container in the cupboard. I combine this flour with others such as white and brown rice or sorghum flour, and the combination works well.

■ POTATO FLOUR

Potato flour and potato starch are confusing. Potato flour is made from cooked potatoes. Potato starch is made from raw potatoes. This flour combines well with rice flours.

■ SORGHUM FLOUR

Sorghum is a gluten-free flour that is very easy to work with. I prefer it to many of the other flours because it so close mimics wheat flour. It is one of the main food crops used in India and Africa, and is creating a huge following in the United States for those with a gluten intolerance. Sorghum flour is high in soluble fiber, and tastes very similar to wheat. When baking with sorghum flour, you will need to add arrowroot or cornstarch to your recipes (1/2 to 1 teaspoon per cup) and also add xanthan gum (1/2 teaspoon per cup) to bind it together. It is great used in cookies, pie crusts, cakes, etc. You will see that I use it in several recipes. I encourage you to try it, too!

■ SOY FLOUR

Soy flour has a very nutty flavor. It is high in fat and also protein. It is yellow in color and has a distinctive taste. I recommend you mix it with other flours, such as rice flour.

It tastes good in products containing nuts and fruits. It does not store well, so buy it in small quantities and store in the refrigerator.

There are many other flours to choose from, including arrowroot flour, cornstarch, and nut and seed flours. I would encourage you to give them a try. All of these substitute flours can be frozen, and the rice flours lasts longer if you keep them in the refrigerator after opening.

MAKING FLOUR SUBSTITUTIONS

IF A RECIPE calls for white or wheat flour, there are many substitutions to choose from. This is encouraging and allows you creativity in the kitchen. If you are new to wheat/gluten alternatives, start small. It may take a while until you find the combinations that work best for you.

When you are substituting flours that have different consistencies, it is important not to use too much, or too little. Here is a brief guide. All of the flours listed below are substitutes for 1 cup of all-purpose (wheat) flour.

- ▶ 1 cup cornstarch
- ▶ $7/8$ cup buckwheat or amaranth flour
- ▶ $1/2$ cup arrowroot or tapioca flour plus $1/2$ cup bean or rice flour
- ▶ $7/8$ cup brown rice or rice flour
- ▶ $3/4$ cup oat flour
- ▶ $1/2$ cup sorghum flour plus $1/2$ cup brown rice flour

There are other substitutions you can use, and I encourage you to experiment. You can also buy premixed flours for baking. Bob's Red Mill brand carries several to choose from.

Where to Find Gluten-, Dairy-, and Sugar-free Products

THE FIRST PLACE I went in search of gluten-free products was our local health food store. They had every kind of gluten-free flour I could want, and I have been very happy with their supplies. I recommend you start there. If you cannot find gluten-free products where you live, the Internet has many resources, and, depending on where you live, supplies are easily obtained through online orders.

ALLERGY RESOURCES, P.O. Box 444, Guffy, CO 80820. They will send you a free catalog.

ARROWHEAD MILLS, Inc. P.O. Box 2059, Hereford, TX 79045, 800-364-0730. Wheat-free grains, beans, oils, flours, mixes, ready-to-eat cereals, butters.

BOB'S RED MILL NATURAL FOODS, 5209 S.E. International Way, Milwaukie, OR 97222, 503-654-3215. Wheat-free, gluten-free flours, pastas, baking mixes, soup mixes, and many other products. Call for a catalog or go to their Web site, www.bobsredmill.com.

BRUMWELL FLOUR MILL, 328 East Second St. Box 233, Sumner, IA 50674, 319-578-8106. Organic flours including oat, corn, and buckwheat. They will also grind unroasted buckwheat if requested.

CELIAC.COM (www.celiac.com) is a wonderful Web site for everything you need to know about avoiding gluten in the diet. They have lists of "forbidden" foods, links to other resources, and a wonderful bookstore, too. If you are allergic to gluten, or need to avoid all products containing gluten, I highly recommend this site. It will provide you with a wealth of information.

DE-RO-MA, 1118 Berlier, Laval, Quebec H7L3R9, 514-990-5694 (Food Intolerance Centre). Gluten-free flours, baking mixes, pastas, cereals. Full catalog available.

EARTH BALANCE, www.earthbalance.net, GFA Brands, Inc. P.O. Box 397, Cresskill, NJ 07626-0397, 201-568-9300. Nonhydrogenated, 100 percent expeller-pressed margarine that is gluten free and dairy free.

ELAM'S, 2625 Gardner Rd., Broadview, IL 60153, 708-865-0116. Grains, flours, snacks, cookies.

ENER-G FOODS, Inc. P.O. Box 84487, Seattle, WA 98124, 800-331-5222. Gluten-free flours, egg-replacer, lactose-free baked breads, soup mixes.

ENJOY LIFE FOODS, www.enjoylifefoods.com, 1601 N. Natchez, Chicago, IL 60707, 888-50-enjoy or 773-889-5070. Many wonderful products, all nut free, dairy free, egg free, soy free, gluten free, GMO free, and kosher. They also will ship bulk agave nectar. Ask for Bert! Tell him Sue sent you.

FOLLOW YOUR HEART VEGAN GOURMET, marick@followyourheart.com Box 9400, Canoga Park, CA 91309-0400, 818-348-3240. Many dairy- and gluten-free cheeses in several flavors.

FOOD FOR LIFE BAKING CO., Inc. P.O. Box 1434, Corona, CA 91718, 800-797-5090. Gluten-free breads, muffins, pasta. Can be found in many natural food stores.

GALAXY FOODS, www.galaxyfoods.com, 2441 Viscount Row, Orlando, FL 32809, 800-808-2325. Specializes in many gluten-free, dairy-free cheeses. Carries a sour cream substitute, as well as many different flavors and textures of cheese alternatives. If you are vegan, check out their alternatives!

THE GREEN EARTH, 2545 Prairie Ave., Evanston, IL 60201, 800-322-3662. Many yeast-free, gluten-free products, organic produce, sweeteners, baby food, organic frozen meats, etc. Will ship all over the United States.

LUNDBERG FAMILY FARMS, www.lundberg.com, P.O. Box 369, Richvale, CA 95974, 916-882-4551. Brown rice, rice cakes, and cereals. (The brown rice syrup that I use in my recipes is this brand. I love it!)

MRS. LEEPER'S PASTA, 12455 Kerran St. #200, Poway, CA 92064. This is my all-time favorite for wheat-free pasta! They carry corn and rice flour pasta, and sauces, too.

ROAD'S END ORGANICS: www.chreese.com, 120 Pleasant St., E-1, Morrisville, VT 05661, 877-247-3373. They carry a nondairy cheese that is made from lentil flour. They also carry various flavors of cheese alternatives, and dips.

SPECTRUM NATURALS, www.spectrumnaturals.com, Spectrum Natural Organic Products, Inc., 5341 Old Redwood Highway, Suite 400, Petaluma, CA 94954, Many wonderful organic products, including nonhydrogenated, trans-fat-free shortening. I use this vegetable shortening in my [wonderful!

Sweet Cactus Farms, agave@sweetcactusfarms.com 10627 [Angeles, CA 90034, 310-733-4343. Vegan, gluten-free su Agave cactus nectar is very low on the glycemic index, and tute for sugar.

Thermosweet, nutrilabcorp@aol.com Customer service, 100 2nd Avenue South, 200 South Tower, St. Petersburg, FL 33701. Manufactures kiwi sweeteners.

Twin Valley Mills, www.twinvalleymills.com, RR 1, Box 45, Ruskin, NE, 68974, 402-279-3965. Sells sorghum flour in bulk.

Vita Soy, USA, Inc., One New England Way, Ayer, MA 01432, 800-vitasoy. They carry a dairy-free, egg-free mayonnaise, Nayonaise, and it is great.

Westbrae Foods, The Hain Celestial Group, 734 Franklin Ave. #444, Garden City, NY 11530, www.westbrae.com, 800-434-4246. Westbraw makes the very best unsweetened un-ketchup and also a fruit-sweetened ketchup. They also carry a very good rice milk.

Wholefoods Market, P.O. Box 244, Gig Harbor, WA 98335, 888-835-2312. They sell 1-gallon containers of agave nectar, as well as many substitute ingredients. Ask for Bruce, and tell him "Suzi" sent you.

Wild Oats, and Fresh Fields Grocery stores all carry a wealth of gluten-free, dairy-free, sugar-free products.

Alternative Ingredients

■ Quinoa

Pronounced "keen-wa," this seed comes from South America. It dates back to the ancient Incan civilization. It is a hearty seed, usually referred to as a grain, containing more protein than any other. The protein found in quinoa is very high quality, and it contains all of the essential amino acids. It is high in linoleic acid, fiber, oil, minerals, vitamins, and starch. It is easy to digest, and has a great nutty flavor. It cooks very quickly, and is easy on the digestive tract. Quinoa is very versatile, and I use it in soups, salads, stuffing, and in place of any grain. Be sure to rinse quinoa well before cooking with it. My favorite recipe in this book is the quinoa stuffing. It's delicious!

■ Oats

Oats are a great source of soluble-rich fiber that boosts energy and helps to lower cholesterol. Oats are grown all over the world, and are high in fiber, protein, and calcium. There are several different types of oats:

Oat Groats

Groats are minimally processed, and only have the outer hull removed. They are chewier, and need to be cooked for a longer period of time, after soaking first.

Steel-cut Oats

I eat this version for breakfast often. Steel-cut oats are known as a "whole grain." They are hearty, great for your heart and lowering cholesterol, and have a nutty flavor that really warms you up and gets you going! They are known by different names, such as Irish oats, Scotch oats, porridge oats, etc. This variety is very chewy and must be cooked for a longer period that rolled oats.

Rolled Oats

Rolled oats are the most common, and have been steamed and rolled to hasten the cooking. They are used for cookies, oatmeal, muesli, and granola.

For many people with celiac disease, or those with dermatitis herpetiformis, oats have been off-limits for many years. Recent literature now indicates that oats may be safe for these individuals, and the only issue that remains is cross-contamination. (Steel-cut oats are said to be the "safest" oats, as they are often processed in plants where no other products are manufactured. Check the labels of your oat products before eating if you have concerns.)

Many doctors still recommend that their patients stay away from oats because it is hard to know for sure if the oats have been contaminated by glutinous products. The U.S. and Canadian Celiac Associations do NOT endorse oats to any celiacs due to the cross-contamination issue. Please check with your doctor before consuming oats. Some recipes in this book contain oats, and you need to check each recipe carefully before preparing if you are not convinced the oats you use are safe.

■ Millet

Millet is a grain rich in protein and minerals. It is easy to cook with, and is good in stews, soups, as cereal, or in breads.

■ Cornstarch and Arrowroot

If you are not allergic to cornstarch, then you can use it in place of flour to thicken sauces and create glazes. Of course, if you are making a gravy or other sauce using meat juices, you can use rice flour to thicken it. I use arrowroot over cornstarch in most recipes. Both of these thickeners work well. If you are using cornstarch, be sure to mix it in a small amount of liquid before adding it to your sauce, as it can develop clumps. I recommend you whisk it thoroughly before adding it in with the rest of the ingredients. Heat until it boils, then reduce the heat and cook until it thickens. Arrowroot works well with acidic fruit sauces, and does not become thin or watery.

■ Baking Soda

I use baking soda in conjunction with baking powder, as alone it will not cause a product to leaven. I use it quite frequently in biscuits, cookies, scones, and the like. It is best if you sift it with the flour and baking powder, as it is somewhat lumpy.

■ Baking Powder

If you are concerned about the health risks of aluminum, you can buy aluminum-free baking powder in health food stores. Ener-G Foods makes a gluten-free baking powder. I use baking powder frequently in my recipes, especially for cakes, cookies, bars, and muffins.

■ BUTTERY SPREAD AND ORGANIC SHORTENING

There is quite a controversy about the health benefits or risks of using margarine. I have found two products that I am very happy with. Earth Balance Natural Shortening works great for cookies, cakes, and muffins. It is non-GMO, trans-fat free, dairy free, and gluten free. Another alternative to butter is Spectrum Naturals Organic Shortening. It, too, is dairy free, and gluten free. It has no cholesterol, and works wonderfully for pie crusts, cookies, cakes, etc. If you are using in to replace butter in a recipe, be sure to blend it at room temperature with your liquid ingredients, such as fruit sweeteners or agave cactus nectar. If the sweetener and the shortening are not at the same temperature, they will not combine well, and they may curdle. I limit the use of these products to baking.

■ VEGETABLE OIL

Oil can be substituted for butter and margarine in recipes. If a recipe calls for oil, I always cut the amount in half, and add unsweetened applesauce to equal the amount required. It keeps the baked item moist, and reduces the amount of fat. I use canola oil or coconut oil in baked goods. I use extra-virgin olive oil for most of my fish and vegetable dishes, as well as in some salad dressings.

■ GRAPESEED OIL

Grapeseed oil is a true treasure. It contains no cholesterol, no trans-fatty acids, no preservatives, is high in antioxidants and vitamin E, and is a great source of lineolic acid. It also contains the highest amounts of monounsaturated and polyunsaturated fats, compared to others. Because of its ability to withstand high heat, it is great for sautéing foods. You can also use it in salad dressings dips, spreads, and much more.

■ COCONUT OIL

Once thought to be bad for us, coconut oil has changed in the minds of researchers. Why? Because coconut oil comes from a plant source, and even though it contains saturated fat, it acts differently than saturated fats from animals. It is made up of medium-chain fatty acids, also known as medium-chain triglycerides. These fatty acids do not contain cholesterol, and in fact have been known to increase metabolism, and promote weight loss. It is heat resistant, making it great to cook with, supports metabolic function, and is reported to supply fewer calories than other fats. Several studies have been done on the medical benefits of this oil, and the results are encouraging. I encourage you to try it.

■ SOY, RICE, OAT, COCONUT, AND ALMOND MILKS

I use soy milk in many of my recipes. It is low in fat and high in protein. I always buy the "unsweetened" versions, as the regular or flavored milks have a very high sugar content. Almond milk is sweet and can be used to replace cow's milk in recipes, too. I like rice milk on cereal for breakfast. I also like to make smoothies for breakfast, and usually include the following: a ripe banana, soy milk, water, and a nondairy frozen dessert, such as Sweet Nothings. It is all-natural and contains no sugar, dairy, gluten, or artificial ingredients. Mango Raspberry is very good! Another option is to add protein powder, or some tofu. To increase the protein in your morning smoothie, add 5 to 6 almonds. Want to increase your fiber? Add 2 to 3 dried figs and ¼ cup frozen or fresh berries, such as raspberries, blueberries, or strawberries.

Rice and soy milk can also be used as a milk substitute in just about everything. Consistency of these milks vary, and you must take that into consideration when looking for a substitute for cow's milk. I would recommend soy or rice milk as a thickener for gravies, but almond milk or coconut milk are delicious as a base for brown rice pudding. Be sure you refrigerate all of these milks after opening, and check the expiration date.

■ EGGS AND EGG SUBSTITUTES

I buy the freshest organic eggs I can find. I use eggs in many of my recipes, but you can use egg substitutes if you are unable to eat eggs. Ener-G Foods makes the best egg substitute I have tried, and there are no egg byproducts in them. I have also used a fat and egg substitute called Wonderslim. It can be used for cooking, baking, and making salad dressings. It is made of water, dried plum juice concentrate, oat fiber, and soy lecithin. It can be found in major health food stores or food co-ops. Marin Food Specialties, Inc. manufactures it; their address is P.O. Box 609 Byron, CA 94514. Be sure you read the instructions on the bottle before adding to your recipes.

You can also use the following substitutions for eggs in a recipe. My favorite is the ground flaxseed, and water.

To replace one egg, use:

- ▶ ¼ cup applesauce
- ▶ 1 tablespoon ground flaxseed plus 3 tablespoons water (this is my favorite egg substitute)
- ▶ 2 tablespoons dried apricots (let stand in water until soft, then puree in a blender).
- ▶ 1 small banana, mashed

I use the ground flaxseeds and water most often, and find the consistency is very similar to eggs, and leaves my baked products very moist.

■ NUTS

I use nuts in many of my recipes. They are a good source of protein, and they also enhance the flavor in recipes. Many recipes call for toasted nuts, such as almonds, pecans, or walnuts. It is not always necessary to toast them but, if time permits, it gives the nuts a earthy flavor. Spread the nuts on a baking sheet and place in a 350°F oven for 8 to 10 minutes. Remove from the oven and cool.

Be sure to store any unused toasted nuts in the refrigerator. You can also freeze them for up to a few months. Be sure to check each recipe if you have a nut allergy, to be sure it does not contain nuts of any kind. I have indicated which recipes have nuts, and which do not. Some recipes may contain peanuts, which are not nuts but legumes.

■ GUAR GUM AND XANTHAN GUM

Guar gum and xanthan gum are used to thicken liquids. You do not have to cook them to have the right effect. I use these products to hold baked goods together. Be sure to use an electric mixer when using these ingredients, for best results.

Guar gum is from the *Cyamopsis tetragonolobus* plant. It is high in fiber, and binds together in baked goods. Xanthan gum is a small organism called *Xanthomonas campestris*. It grows a special coating, which is removed in the chemical process. It is then dried and milled, and eventually becomes a powder. There are approximately 8 calories in each tablespoon. It is used to substitute gluten in breads and baked goods.

OTHER FOODS TO AVOID

THESE FOODS ARE considered "not safe" for those adhering to a gluten-free diet.

Ale, beer, kamut, spelt, wheat germ, canned meats, cold cuts, hot dogs (unless guaranteed pure meat), gravies, malt, brewer's yeast, bulgur wheat, soy sauce, teriyaki sauce, barley, textured vegetable protein, semolina flour, food starch, graham flour, bran, couscous.

DINING OUT

IF YOU ARE a person who does not eat sugar, dairy, and gluten, this is a challenge. It is not impossible to enjoy a healthy meal in a restaurant, but it takes a commitment to your health. There are so many temptations placed before us in restaurants, such as breads, butters, etc. Be sure when ordering that you tell your food server you have food allergies, or just notify the food-server that you do not want any gluten, dairy, or sugar in your meal. I ask the food-servers many questions about the dishes on the menu, and how they are prepared. I am amazed at how many dishes are prepared with gluten, in one form or another. Gravies, sauces, breading, and even dressings can contain wheat or gluten, so it is important to ask. Salads are a pretty safe bet. You can always be safe by ordering an oil-and-vinegar dressing, but some vinaigrettes can also be fine. It is usually safe to ask for grilled fish or meat, steamed vegetables, or clear soups. Baked potatoes or sweet potatoes are also a safe food. Many restaurants these days are conscious of food allergies. Most offer special meals for people wishing to avoid gluten, sugar, and dairy.

I find that many restaurants will cater to your needs, if you ask. It may depend on how busy the place is at the time, and whether the establishment has a policy about substitutions. I always ask about the vegetables or starch that accompanies the meal, and how they are prepared. It is often an awkward situation, so I always prepare my dining partners that I will have to ask several questions about the meal. I have found that I can often substitute more vegetables for the starch, or I have more salad instead of a starch.

If at all possible, try to find restaurants that cater to the health-oriented customer. That makes your choices greater, and your service is often more accommodating as well.

I avoid fast-food restaurants as there is little I can or want to eat there. Many of them are changing their menus to be more accommodating, but they still don't offer many gluten-free, dairy-free, or sugar-free alternatives.

This is unrelated to gluten or sugar, but farmed salmon is another food to avoid. Farmed fish are given antibiotics, hormones, and dyes to produce the pink color found in wild salmon. They are raised in pens, not in the wild, and are labeled "Atlantic Salmon." Beware, farmed fish contains more harmful ingredients than health benefits!

When I am invited to a dinner party or family function, I try to bring something I know I can eat. I volunteer to bring a main dish, side dish, or salad, and that way I know I will, at the very least, be able to eat what I have brought. It is difficult when you are the only guest who has to eliminate specific foods, so I may or may not tell the host or hostess of my dietary needs. I try to eat what I can, and if I know I will not be able to eat anything served, I eat before I go.

The recipes in this book will fool everyone. They taste great. I have served these recipes to those who eat wheat, sugar, and dairy, and they have told me they can't tell any difference. To me, that has been the greatest compliment I have received. That has been my goal: to prepare recipes that are free from gluten, sugar, and dairy, in many cases, but that also taste good and are easy to make. If I have provided you with a cookbook full of good-tasting recipes that even the most critical of critics enjoys, then I have done my job well.

What Is the Glycemic Index?

THE GLYCEMIC INDEX is a way of measuring the carbohydrate content of a food. Foods high in carbohydrates, such as white flour, white potatoes, white rice, are very high on the glycemic index, and cause a rapid increase in blood sugar. Not all carbohydrates are the same, as some are digested very quickly in the intestine, causing blood sugar to rise rapidly, and others, such as raw cherries, grapefruit, or kiwi are very low on the glycemic scale and do not cause a rapid response of insulin from the pancreas.

If you are trying to eat a healthy diet, it is good to consume foods that are lower on the glycemic index scale, to keep your blood sugars balanced. All foods have a number that indicates their glycemic index. Those foods with highest numbers cause the greatest rise in blood sugars, and those with lower numbers, a smaller rise in blood sugar levels. There are many sites on the Internet that offer information about the glycemic index, as well as the index scale itself. If you are concerned with the amount of carbohydrates you are consuming, and wish to lower your intake of high-glycemic carbs, look to the Internet for more information. There are also books available on this topic, such as *The New Glucose Revolution: The Authoritative Guide to the Glycemic Index*. This book was co-authored by Jennie Brand-Miller, PhD and Thomas M. S. Wolever, MD, PhD. *The Good Carb Cookbook: Secrets of Eating Low on the Glycemic Index* by Sandra L. Woodruff is another. *The South Beach Diet* by Dr. Arthur Agatston is another book that touts foods low on the glycemic index, not only to help those who wish to lose weight, but to support a healthier cardiovascular system.

Buying Organic

MANY PEOPLE ARE affected by toxins, and chemicals in our environment. In our homes we have cleansers that are hazardous to our health, and our foods are grown with pesticides or hormones, or are genetically modified. I recommend not only that you think about the foods you buy, but also about the products you use in your home. If we are going to make our health better by eating better, we also need to pay attention to the types of cleaning supplies and fertilizers we buy. I believe we can use nontoxic products to keep our homes clean, or yards healthy, and our appearance beautiful, from the inside out.

I buy organic food whenever I can. I prefer to eat food that I know is free of toxic chemicals. In the case of animals, I know that animals raised on organic farms are not given drugs such as antibiotics or hormones. Organic produce is not genetically modified in any way, and the method used to grow the produce is done in an ecological balance of natural systems.

If the label says 100 percent organic, the products must be completely organic. Some foods state they are "organic" but they may contain up to 5 percent of nonorganic substances. Only 100 percent organic contains all organic ingredients. I do not specify that each ingredient should be organic in my recipes, but when you can buy organic, I hope you will.

Weight Loss

THIS BOOK DOES not claim to be a weight-loss book. I have worked as a food management consultant over the years, helping people find alternatives to various foods, and many of those people reported losing weight after making a change in their diets. I believe if you reduce the number of calories you consume, and increase your activity, you will lose weight. If you read the current diet books on the market, they tell you to balance your diet, eating smaller amounts of fat and carbs, and increasing the amount of protein. They also stress exercise as part of a weight-loss plan.

The new thinking out there in the weight-loss world is, "no white flour, white bread, white sugar, white rice." I have heard doctors say on TV, on the radio, and in magazines, "Don't eat anything white and you will lose weight." The theory is, as I understand it, that those foods (white bread, white sugar, white rice) are "simple carbohydrates" and turn to sugar rapidly in the body, and do not contain much nutritional value. They are also very high on the glycemic index scale. The way to improve your health is to eat complex carbohydrates, whole grains, smaller, and more frequent meals; avoid junk food; and move more. Then you will truly live your best life!

This book is gluten free. No white flour in this book. No white sugar in this book. No refined anything in this book. I recommend only the healthiest ingredients, and do not recommend processed foods. I make everything from scratch, and I feel that this is the healthiest way to eat. I believe the energy you put into preparing your food will provide you with the energy you need to live a healthy life.

If I have listed white rice in a recipe, and you want to avoid "simple carbohydrates," please feel free to replace the white rice with brown rice, red rice (my favorite), or another rice of your choice. Lentil rice has more protein, and is a wonderful substitute for regular rice. The problem I have is finding it! You will need to ask your health food store if they have it, or can find it for you.

Here are some healthy alternatives for a less healthy snack that you may now enjoy:

- ▶ a handful of nuts (almonds or walnuts are best)
- ▶ hummus dip plus sliced red bell peppers or carrot sticks (I like apples dipped in hummus, too!)
- ▶ celery stuffed with peanut butter
- ▶ apples with peanut butter spread on top, and you can add to this, too, such as with raisins, or nuts
- ▶ popcorn
- ▶ soy nuts
- ▶ turkey jerky
- ▶ hard-boiled or deviled eggs
- ▶ guacamole with veggies
- ▶ fresh fruits or berries
- ▶ protein drink
- ▶ applesauce
- ▶ gorp, or a mixture of nuts, seeds, dried fruits, etc.
- ▶ smoothies

As I said earlier, this book is not written as a weight-loss book, but if you choose to eliminate gluten products and refined sugars from your diet, I am confident you will notice a difference, not only in how you feel, but how you look as well.

breakfast dishes

Breakfast Muesli

NO EGGS

PREP TIME: 2 hours with chilling time included
SERVE: Serves 5

This dish is addictive, so be careful. *My cooking students loved this recipe so much most of them went home and made a batch right away. It stores well in the refrigerator for several days but I doubt it will last that long.*

1 cup oats or brown rice flakes
¼ cup quinoa flour
1 cup nonfat yogurt/soy yogurt
½ cup soy milk
¼ cup agave nectar
½ cup chopped walnuts
3 tablespoons chopped dates
3 tablespoons sesame seeds
3 tablespoons currants
Blueberries, raspberries, or
   strawberries

- Combine all of the ingredients except the berries in a large bowl, and mix well. Add more yogurt if you prefer a thinner muesli. Cover and place in the refrigerator for at least 2 hours. Top with the berries before serving.

- This recipe can be altered by adding other fruit, such as peaches in place of the berries. You can also take out the dates and add dried cranberries, cherries, or whatever you prefer. Use your imagination!

nutritional analysis per serving
344.94 calories; 13.05 g fat (32% calories from fat); 10.88 g protein; 51.39 g carbohydrate; 0.40 mg cholesterol; 18.36 mg sodium

Breakfast Quinoa

NO DAIRY OR EGGS

PREP TIME: 30 minutes
SERVE: Serves 4

You can do a lot with this recipe. Omit the oats and use quinoa flakes. Take out the nuts and add sesame or sunflower seeds. Add fresh berries or chopped apples. Experiment! This is chock full of protein, and will give you a great boost in the morning!

½ cup quinoa, rinsed and drained

1 cup water

½ cup oats or quinoa flakes

½ cup chopped peaches

2 tablespoons blackstrap molasses or agave nectar

¼ cup chopped walnuts (optional)

¼ cup chopped dates, raisins, or currants,

■ Place the quinoa in a saucepan with the water and bring to a boil. Reduce the heat and simmer until done, about 10 minutes. Add the oats or quinoa flakes, peaches, molasses, chopped nuts, and chopped dates, and simmer for 10 to 15 minutes, or until light and fluffy. Serve hot.

nutritional analysis per serving
236.39 calories; 6.72 g fat (24% calories from fat); 5.92 g protein; 40.80 g carbohydrate; 0 mg cholesterol; 10.43 mg sodium

Buckwheat Pancakes
with Blueberry Sauce

NO DAIRY OR NUTS

PREP TIME: 15 minutes to prepare and 15 minutes to cook
SERVE: Serves 6

I enjoy a good pancake now and again, and I think you will find these scrumptious. If you prefer dairy to soy, go ahead and make that change straight across. I have not tried other milks, such as rice or hazelnut, but they would work, if you adjust the flours, as those milks are not as thick as soy. You can serve with syrup if you wish, but I really like the berry sauce.

Pancakes:

1½ cups soymilk

½ cup unsweetened applesauce

2 eggs, or 2 tablespoons Ener-G egg replacer

1 teaspoon vanilla extract

2 tablespoons grapeseed or canola oil

1 tablespoon agave nectar

1 cup buckwheat flour

½ cup sorghum flour

2 teaspoons baking powder

1 teaspoon ground cinnamon

Sauce:

3 tablespoons orange juice

2 cups blueberries

2 tablespoons arrowroot

⅛ cup agave nectar or fruit sweetener

¼ teaspoon ground cinnamon

- In a large mixing bowl, combine the milk, applesauce, eggs, vanilla, oil, and agave, beating well. Set aside. In a smaller bowl, combine the flours, baking powder, and cinnamon. Add to the liquid ingredients and stir well. Heat a skillet over medium heat and cook each pancake until done. Add more milk, or a small amount of water if you prefer a thinner pancake.
- To make the sauce: Combine the orange juice, cinnamon, blueberries, arrowroot and agave nectar in a small saucepan. Bring to a boil. Lower the heat and simmer for 5 to 6 minutes, or until thick.
- Pour the blueberry sauce over the pancakes.
- Serve warm.

nutritional analysis per serving
271.40 calories; 8.64 g fat (28% calories from fat); 8.67 g protein; 41.29 g carbohydrate; 70.05 mg cholesterol; 58.24 mg sodium

Jeffrey's Egg Scramble

PREP TIME: 30 to 35 minutes
SERVE: Serves 4

I had to name this recipe after my son because it is his all-time favorite breakfast dish. Whenever we are together, he asks me to prepare it. When I make it for him, I use real bacon, but prosciutto works well, too.

6 slices turkey or pork bacon (optional), chopped

2 tablespoons canola or grapeseed oil

3 cups red potatoes, washed cubed

1 large red onion, chopped finely

1 red bell pepper, chopped

2 cloves garlic, minced

⅛ cup milk or soy milk

6 large eggs, beaten slightly

2 large egg whites, beaten slightly

1 cup Cheddar cheese or vegan cheese, grated

½ teaspoon salt

¼ teaspoon freshly ground pepper

Fresh parsley

- Heat a large skillet and cook the bacon over medium heat for 4 to 5 minutes. Drain and set aside.
- In a large skillet, heat the oil and add the potatoes. Sauté over medium heat for 10 to 12 minutes, or until slightly tender. Add the onion, red bell pepper, and garlic. Continue to sauté until the onion is soft and the potatoes are tender, about 5 to 10 minutes.
- In a medium-size bowl combine the milk, beaten eggs, and egg whites.
- Add the bacon to the skillet with the vegetables and pour the egg mixture on top. Cook over medium heat, gently lifting up sections of the egg mixture to be sure the eggs are reaching the heat underneath. Cover with a lid and lower the heat to medium-low. Continue to cook until the eggs are set. Add the cheese, cover, and let the cheese melt.
- Season with salt and pepper, and add fresh parsley, if desired.

nutritional analysis per serving
418.09 calories; 23.07 g fat (49% calories from fat); 25.90 g protein; 26.85 g carbohydrate; 371.41 mg cholesterol; 894.83 mg sodium

Multi-Grain Pancakes

PREP TIME: 20 minutes, including cooking time.
SERVE: Serves 6

I used to make these pancakes before the kids left for a ski trip or other sporting event. They are hearty, and give them the nutritional start they needed for a day of physical exertion. If you don't want to include oats, try millet flakes or quinoa flakes (will add more protein) or brown rice flakes. These pancakes will fill you up with energy.

1 cup buckwheat flour

¼ cup oats

2 tablespoons cornmeal

1½ teaspoons baking powder

½ teaspoon salt

2 tablespoons fruit sweetener or cactus nectar

1 cup soy milk

2 tablespoons oil

1 large egg

- Heat a griddle. Combine the dry ingredients. Stir well. In a separate bowl, combine all the other ingredients. Beat until well mixed. Add the dry ingredients to wet ingredients and stir until smooth. Spoon about ¼-cup batter for each pancake onto the griddle. Cook for about 2 minutes each side.
- Serve with sugar-free maple syrup, all-fruit jam, yogurt, or margarine.

> Note: If you wish to use dairy, decrease the oil by 1 tablespoon and add 1/4-cup nonfat plain yogurt.

nutritional analysis per serving
179.28 calories; 7.27 g fat (35% calories from fat); 5.85 g protein; 25.61 g carbohydrate; 35.25 mg cholesterol; 335.48 mg sodium

Scrambled Eggs and Tofu

PREP TIME: 30 minutes
SERVE: Serves 4

This is a quick, easy breakfast that provides a good dose of protein. It is great leftover and can be easily jazzed up by adding other herbs and spices. Feel free to use up other veggies on hand, too, such as broccoli or mushrooms. This is really just the foundation; you can add to this recipe using up leftovers in the fridge.

1 tablespoons olive oil

½ small red onion, chopped

3 cloves garlic, minced

½ medium-size zucchini, sliced

½ cup red bell pepper, chopped

2 eggs

½ pound firm tofu, drained and chopped

¼ teaspoon dried rosemary or basil (optional)

Salt and pepper to taste

- Heat the oil in a skillet. Add the onion, garlic, zucchini, and pepper. Sauté until the vegetables begin to soften. Beat the eggs in a small bowl. Add the tofu and eggs to the vegetables, and cook for 1 to 2 minutes or until cooked.
- Add the rosemary or basil and the seasonings, and heat through.

nutritional analysis per serving
144.46 calories; 9.91 g fat (60% calories from fat); 10.27 g protein; 5.28 g carbohydrate; 122.67 mg cholesterol; 121.89 mg sodium

breads
and muffins

Gingerbread

PREP TIME: about 10 minutes to prepare and about 20 minutes to bake
SERVE: Serves 9

This gingerbread is so good, just like grandma used to make—minus the sugar. To reduce the amount of fat, if that is an issue for you, decrease the eggs to 1 egg and use 1 tablespoon of ground flaxseeds mixed with 3 table-spoons of water. If you prefer to eliminate the eggs all together, try Ener-G Foods egg substitute—it's very good. This bread is so tasty, it won't last long around your house, I guarantee it.

½ cup pecans or walnuts, chopped finely

½ cup agave nectar or fruit sweetener

¼ cup canola oil

2 eggs

½ teaspoon grated orange rind

1 teaspoon vanilla extract

1½ cups brown rice flour or sorghum flour

½ teaspoon salt

1 teaspoon baking powder

1 teaspoon baking soda

2 teaspoons ground ginger

1½ teaspoon ground cinnamon

¼ teaspoon grated nutmeg

⅛ teaspoon cloves

1 cup unsweetened applesauce

- In a large mixing bowl, combine the agave nectar and oil. Beat on high speed until thoroughly blended. You can use fruit sweetener if you prefer, but I really like the agave nectar in this recipe. After you have mixed the oil and sweetener, add the eggs, one at a time. Be sure to beat well between additions. Add the orange rind and vanilla and continue to blend together. Set aside.
- Meanwhile, preheat the oven to 350°F, spray a 9-inch square pan with a non-stick spray and prepare the dry ingredients.
- Sift together the dry ingredients and add the nuts to them.
- Now, add some of the dry ingredients to the wet ingredients, a little at a time, blending well. Add ¼ cup of the applesauce, blend, then add more of the dry mixture. Continue until you have added all the ingredients.
- Pour the batter into the pan and bake for 20 to 25 minutes, or until the gingerbread is done. Check for doneness by inserting a toothpick, or touching lightly on the center. If it leaves an indent, the gingerbread is not done. If it springs back, remove to a cooling rack.
- This gingerbread freezes well.

> If you need to avoid eggs, substitute Ener-G egg substitute or read the suggestions for substitutions at the beginning of the book.

nutritional analysis per serving
268.56 calories; 12.13 g fat (39% calories from fat); 3.82 g protein; 39.10 g carbohydrate; 54.52 mg cholesterol; 342.08 mg sodium

Mexican Cornbread

PREP TIME: 15 minutes to prepare and 45 to 50 minutes to bake
SERVE: Serves 4

This is a fun bread to make, as you can add to it to give it more color and texture. Try adding some black olives, scallions, or jalapeño peppers. (If you add olives, use ⅛ cup sliced olives.) Store this bread in an airtight container in the refrigerator. You'll find it a pleasant complement to any Mexican dish.

8 ounces creamed corn
½ cup salsa
½ cup soymilk
⅛ cup canola oil
2 large eggs, lightly beaten
1 cup cornmeal
2 teaspoons baking powder
½ teaspoon sea salt
2 cups Cheddar cheese
4 ounces green chiles, chopped
Vegetable oil spray

- Preheat the oven to 350°F
- Mix all ingredients together in a large bowl. Spoon into a 9-inch square pan that has been sprayed with a vegetable oil and bake at 350°F in the preheated oven for 45 to 50 minutes, or until the top is golden brown.
- Serve with beans and rice.

> You can also use nondairy cheese in place of the cheese, if you wish.

nutritional analysis per serving
319.74 calories; 14.66 g fat (23% calories from fat); 9.28 g protein; 40.46 g carbohydrate; 123.24 mg cholesterol; 734.18 mg sodium

My Favorite Banana Nut Bread

NO DAIRY

PREP TIME: 10 minutes to prepare and 60 minutes to bake
SERVE: Serves 8

Your kids will love this bread. It's easy to make and tastes delicious. It's a great bread to pack in school lunches. Works well for your neighborhood tea party, too.

¼ cup agave nectar

¼ cup canola oil

¼ cup unsweetened applesauce

2 large eggs, beaten

1 teaspoon vanilla extract

2 tablespoons water

1⅓ cups mashed bananas

1½ cups brown rice flour

¾ cup quinoa flour

¼ cup arrowroot

1 tablespoon baking powder

½ teaspoon salt

¼ cup chopped walnuts

- Preheat the oven to 350°F
- In a large mixing bowl, cream the agave nectar and canola oil until they are well mixed. Add the applesauce and mix until blended. Add the eggs, vanilla, and water. Mix well after each addition. Add mashed bananas and set aside. The mixture will look curdled.
- In a separate bowl, stir together the flours, arrowroot, baking powder, and salt. Add this mixture to the banana mixture and stir to combine. Add the nuts and pour into a greased 8 × 4-inch loaf pan. Bake for 1 hour at 350°F. Be sure to test the bread about 50 minutes into the baking process, as cooking times vary depending on your oven.
- Cool on a wire rack.

nutritional analysis per serving
249.25 calories; 10.76 g fat (40% calories from fat); 4.06 g protein; 35.28 g carbohydrate; 52.88 mg cholesterol; 350.43 mg sodium

Potato Scones

PREP TIME: 45 minutes
SERVE: Serves 6

I love yams and they would work nicely in place of the potatoes for a colorful addition. To change this recipe up a bit, omit the rosemary and add chives in its place and a pinch of nutmeg. These scones are wonderful served with lamb or pork, or simply by themselves.

1 pound potatoes, peeled, washed, and quartered

1 cup sorghum flour

½ teaspoon gluten-free baking powder

3 tablespoons olive oil

2 green onions, chopped finely

1 tablespoon fresh rosemary

Canola oil, for frying

½ teaspoon salt

¼ teaspoon pepper

- Steam or boil the potatoes until soft. Mash well and add the flour, baking powder, olive oil, onions, rosemary, and seasonings. (You can substitute other herbs for the rosemary if you prefer.) Stir well.
- Roll out on a floured board. The dough should be about ¼-inch thick.
- Cut rounds with a pastry cutter or an inverted drinking glass. Heat a skillet over medium-high heat and heat a tablespoon of the canola oil. Cook on each side for about 5 minutes, or until lightly browned. Turn only once per scone. Continue this process, adding a tablespoon of oil at a time and the scones. Keep the scones warm in the oven until all have been prepared.
- I serve this recipe with lamb, and top the scones with caper sauce. They are delicious!
- You can also serve them with eggs or as a side dish with pork, chicken, or other meats.

nutritional analysis per serving
203.59 calories; 14.00 g fat (61% calories from fat); 1.55 g protein; 18.49 g carbohydrate; 0 mg cholesterol; 199.47 mg sodium

Pumpkin Bread

PREP TIME: 10 minutes to prepare and 60 minutes to bake
SERVE: Serves 8

If you can't find currants, you can substitute raisins or even chopped dates in this recipe. This is a great fall or winter treat, and won't last long as it is very good. Store in an airtight container to maintain freshness.

2 cups sorghum flour

½ teaspoon ground cinnamon

½ teaspoon grated nutmeg

½ teaspoon salt

2 teaspoons baking powder

1 teaspoon. baking soda

¼ cup vegetable oil

½ cup agave nectar or fruit sweetener

½ cup unsweetened applesauce

2 eggs

¾ cup canned organic pumpkin

½ cup pecans, chopped

1 cup currants

- Preheat the oven to 350°F
- In a medium-size bowl, combine all the dry ingredients and mix well. Set aside.
- In a large mixing bowl, mix together the oil and agave nectar, and beat until well blended. Add the applesauce and eggs, alternating between the two ingredients. When they are well blended, add the pumpkin.
- Add the dry ingredients to the wet and mix on low speed until they are blended, but do not overbeat. Add the nuts and currants, and pour into a greased and floured bread pan. Bake at 350°F for about 1 hour.
- To check the bread for doneness, insert a toothpick in the center—if it comes out clean, the bread is done. Cool on a wire rack for about 10 minutes, then remove from the pan and continue cooling.

nutritional analysis per serving
234.81 calories; 13.45 g fat (50% calories from fat); 3.78 g protein; 27.78 g carbohydrate; 61.33 mg cholesterol; 406.94 mg sodium

Blueberry Muffins

NO DAIRY, EGGS, OR NUTS

PREP TIME: 10 minutes to prepare and up to 20 minutes to bake
SERVE: Serves 6

These muffins are best eaten within a few days of baking them They will hold over in the refrigerator a few days longer, but they are so good, I doubt they will last that long. You can replace the blueberries with chopped apples or raspberries.

¼ cup canola oil

3 tablespoons agave nectar

¼ cup applesauce

¼ cup water

1 teaspoon vanilla extract

1 cup sorghum or brown rice flour

½ cup arrowroot

1 tablespoon baking powder

¼ teaspoon salt

1 teaspoon orange zest

½ cup blueberries

- Preheat the oven to 375°F
- In a large bowl or electric mixer, combine the oil and agave nectar. Beat until smooth. Add the applesauce, water, and vanilla. Beat well.
- In a separate bowl, combine the flour, arrowroot, baking powder, and salt, and mix well. Add to the liquid ingredients and mix until well blended. Fold in the orange rind and blueberries. Do not overbeat. Pour into greased muffin pans and bake for 18 to 20 minutes at 375°F.

nutritional analysis per serving
181.81 calories; 9.31 g fat (45% calories from fat);
0.15 g protein; 26.42 g carbohydrate; 0 mg cholesterol;
586.13 mg sodium

Breakfast Muffins

NO DAIRY

PREP TIME: 20 minutes to prepare and 20 to 25 minutes to bake
SERVE: Serves 6 (makes 6 large muffins)

You can substitute any gluten-/wheat-free cereal for the millet flakes in this recipe. It's best to eat them up quickly, as they won't last at room temperature for more than a few days. You can freeze them in zip-top bags.

⅓ cup garbanzo bean flour

⅓ cup tapioca flour

⅓ cup arrowroot powder

¼ cup gluten-free millet flakes, crushed

1½ teaspoons ground cinnamon

¼ teaspoon grated nutmeg

½ teaspoon baking soda

1½ teaspoons baking powder

½ teaspoon salt

¼ cup vegetable oil

¼ cup agave nectar

2 eggs

½ cup carrots, grated

½ cup unsweetened applesauce

½ cup chopped apple

¼ cup walnuts, chopped finely

⅓ cup dates or dried cranberries, chopped

- Preheat the oven to 400°F. Spray large muffin tins with vegetable oil spray.
- Combine the flours, arrowroot, millet flakes, cinnamon, nutmeg, baking soda, baking powder, and salt. Blend well. Set aside. In a mixing bowl, beat together the oil and agave nectar until fluffy. Add the eggs and beat well. Add the grated carrots, applesauce, and grated apple. Stir. Combine with the dry ingredients. Add the walnuts and dates. Mix until blended, but do not overbeat. Fill cups two-thirds full. Bake for 20 to 25 minutes. Remove from the oven and cool on a wire rack.

nutritional analysis per serving
244.09 calories; 13.93 g fat (49% calories from fat); 3.72 g protein; 28.60 g carbohydrate; 72.0 mg cholesterol; 229.0 mg sodium

Date-Nut Muffins

PREP TIME: 10 minutes to prepare and up to 20 minutes to bake
SERVE: Serves 6

These delicious muffins can be made with raisins in place of the dates, and with pecans instead of the walnuts if you prefer. They are very moist and make a wonderful addition to your brunch on Sunday morning or breakfast any day of the week.

½ cup butter (or buttery spread)
¼ cup agave nectar
1 large egg
1 cup yogurt (or soy yogurt)
¼ cup water
¾ cup brown rice flour
¾ cup sorghum flour
½ teaspoon salt
½ teaspoon grated nutmeg
2 teaspoons baking powder
½ cup dates, chopped
½ cup walnuts, chopped
½ teaspoon ground cinnamon

- Preheat the oven to 375°F.
- In a large mixing bowl, beat the butter and agave until creamy. Add the egg and beat until well blended. Add the yogurt and water, and mix well. Set aside.
- In a large bowl, sift together the brown rice flour, sorghum flour, salt, nutmeg, and baking powder. Add to the moist ingredients and stir until just blended. Do not overbeat. Stir in the dates, walnuts, and cinnamon, and then spoon into muffin pans. (I don't use paper liners, but you can. I prefer to spray the muffin pans with a vegetable oil.)
- Bake at 375°F for 15 to 20 minutes, or until lightly browned. Cool on wire racks.

> **Can be made dairy free.**

nutritional analysis per serving
226.47 calories; 17.12 g fat (66% of calories from fat); 3.87 g protein; 20.55 g carbohydrate; 78.37 mg cholesterol; 399.71 mg sodium

Sweet Potato Biscuits

PREP TIME: 7–45 minutes to prepare yams, 30 minutes for preparation and baking
SERVE: Serves 6

I created these biscuits as a treat for my cooking class students. They loved them. You can also substitute organic pumpkin for the yams, and even use this same recipe to make scones by adding some chopped dates and a squeeze of fresh orange juice.

2 large yams (enough to make ¾ cup yam puree)

1 cup sorghum flour

¼ cup arrowroot powder

¼ cup potato starch

¼ cup brown rice flour

1 teaspoon xantham gum

2 teaspoons baking powder

1 teaspoon baking soda

¼ teaspoon grated nutmeg

6 tablespoons butter or shortening

1 tablespoon agave nectar

1 egg

⅓ cup soy milk (or cow's milk if you prefer dairy biscuits)

- Place the yams directly on the oven rack and bake at 350°F until soft. Remove from the oven and let cool. Peel off the skins and puree the yams until smooth. You should have ¾ cup yam puree.
- In a large bowl, mix together the flours, xantham gum, baking powder, baking soda, and arrowroot powder. Cut in the butter until the dough resembles small peas.
- In another bowl, mix the agave with the egg and soymilk. Add to the dry ingredients.
- Add the yam puree and mix well.
- Preheat the oven to 425°F.
- Roll out the dough on floured board, and cut into biscuits, using either a biscuit cutter or drinking glass. Place on cookie sheet and bake 15 to 20 minutes or until a toothpick in the center comes out clean. Let cool on a wire rack.

> To reduce fat, decrease oil by half and add 3 tablespoons applesauce.

nutritional analysis per serving
308.43 calories; 14.057 g fat (40.5% calories from fat); 4.31 g protein; 38.74 g carbohydrate; 67.57 mg cholesterol; 107.15 mg sodium

appetizers

Baba Ghanouj

NO DAIRY OR NUTS

PREP/COOK TIME: 1 hour
SERVE: Serves 8

If you love eggplants, you'll love this appetizer. I like to serve it with veggies or rice crackers. It tastes great served on top of a baked potato or yam.

2 medium-size eggplants, peeled

¼ cup sesame tahini

3 cloves garlic, crushed

¼ cup chopped fresh parsley

2 tablespoons lemon juice

½ teaspoon ground cumin

1 teaspoon salt

Black pepper to taste

1 tablespoon olive oil

- Preheat the oven to 400°F.
- Prepare the eggplants for baking by cutting off the stems and pricking them all over with a fork. Place them directly on the oven rack and bake at 400°F until they are soft and wrinkled. This should take 40 to 45 minutes. Do NOT place them on a cookie sheet; it is important to place them directly on the oven rack. Carefully remove them from the oven and let them cool for a few minutes.
- While the eggplants are cooling, combine the sesame tahini, garlic, parsley, lemon juice, cumin, salt, and pepper in a blender. Puree. Add the cooled eggplants and continue to puree until smooth.
- Drizzle the olive oil on top and season with more ground pepper.

nutritional analysis per serving
67.68 calories; 5.74 g fat (72% calories from fat);
1.64 g protein; 3.62 g carbohydrate; 0 mg cholesterol;
294.28 mg sodium

Cottage Cheese Dip

PREP TIME: 15 minutes
SERVE: Serves 4

This appetizer can be jazzed up by adding jalapeño pepper, red pepper flakes, or cucumbers. Start with this as the base, and add your favorite flavors. You could add olives, sun-dried tomatoes, and cream cheese, or whatever else pleases your taste buds.

1 cup low-fat cottage cheese

¼ cup nonfat plain yogurt

⅓ cup hummus

1 tablespoon lemon juice

2 teaspoons minced green onions

Salt and pepper, to taste

■ Place the cottage cheese and yogurt in a blender, and mix until smooth. Add the hummus; blend until well mixed. Add the lemon juice and green onions, and stir to mix. Add salt and pepper to taste. Serve.

nutritional analysis per serving
105.49 calories; 3.57 g fat (29% calories from fat); 11.04 g protein; 7.37 g carbohydrate; 6.39 mg cholesterol; 330.03 mg sodium

Deviled Eggs

PREP TIME: 15 to 20 minutes
SERVE: Serves 6

This recipe came from my mom, and
it was a family favorite. You can do so
much with this recipe to give it some
kick, such as adding a dash of cayenne
pepper or curry powder. You can also
try adding some smoked salmon,
olives, or capers.

6 hard-boiled eggs

2–3 tablespoons mayonnaise

1 teaspoon Dijon mustard, or ½
    teaspoon dry mustard

½ teaspoon salt

Pepper, to taste

½ teaspoon dried parsley

Paprika

■ Cut the hard-boiled eggs in half very carefully.
Place the yolks in a small bowl and add the
mayonnaise, mustard, parsley, salt, and pepper. Mix well. Fill the eggshells with the yolk
mixture and sprinkle with the paprika.

nutritional analysis per serving
109.26 calories; 7.72 g fat (63% of calories from fat);
7.26 g protein; 2.37 g carbohydrate; 242.42 g cholesterol; 115.97 mg sodium

Dorothy's Artichoke Nibbles

NO NUTS

PREP TIME: 10 minutes to prepare and 30 to 35 to bake
SERVE: Serves 12

My mother made this recipe for every Thanksgiving and Christmas. We loved them! They are great for any large gathering. If you wish to make this dairy free, be careful when buying non-dairy cheese. Be sure it is casein free. If you can find a "sharp" cheese substitute, that will work best in this recipe.

2 6-ounce jars artichoke hearts, packed in oil, drained and chopped into chunks

1 small onion, chopped finely

1 clove garlic, minced

4 eggs, beaten

¼ cup rice cracker crumbs

¼ teaspoon salt

⅛ teaspoon pepper

¼ teaspoon dried oregano

⅛ teaspoon Tabasco

2 cups Cheddar or vegan cheese

- Preheat the oven to 325°F.
- Combine all ingredients in a large mixing bowl. Mix until well blended. Pour ingredients into a 9-inch square pan and bake at 325°F for 30 to 35 minutes.

> This recipe is wonderful with the addition of 1 cup of cracked crab.

nutritional analysis per serving
129.06 calories; 9.02 g fat (62% of calories from fat); 8.40 g protein; 3.86 g carbohydrate; 93.60 g cholesterol; 234.36 mg sodium

Hummus

NO DAIRY, EGGS, OR NUTS

PREP TIME: 20 minutes
SERVE: Serves 6

Another wonderful party dish, this recipe stores well in the refrigerator for snacking with rice crackers or veggies. I have used this as a spread, placed a large dollop on top of a baked yam, or served it on top of sliced apples. It is full of protein, and is a great snack food for kids, too. Stuff some celery with it, and send it off in their lunch boxes.

4 cloves garlic
1 tablespoon olive oil
1 (15-ounce) can chickpeas
4 tablespoons sesame tahini
3 tablespoons water
1 teaspoon salt
¼ cup lemon juice
½ teaspoon pepper
2 tablespoons chopped fresh
   parsley (optional)
½ teaspoon ground cumin

■ Preheat the oven to 400°F. Place the garlic in a small baking dish and drizzle the olive oil over the top. Do not remove the skins. Bake for about 15 minutes, or until soft. Cool, then remove the skins and add the garlic to the blender with the rest of the ingredients. Blend until smooth. Add more water if the mixture is too thick.

> You can do a lot with hummus. Be creative!

nutritional analysis per serving
176.16 calories; 8.48 g fat (41% calories from fat); 5.77 g protein; 21.07 g carbohydrate; 0 mg cholesterol; 250.17 mg sodium

Roasted Veggie Dip

PREP TIME: 60 minutes
SERVE: Serves 8

A word of warning: Keep an eye on the veggies when they are roasting, as oven heat varies, and you want them roasted but not burned beyond use. Feel free to add other herbs to this recipe, such as basil, tarragon, or rosemary. This tastes great over baked potatoes or yams. I also like to serve it with veggies at parties.

2 small, firm tomatoes, chopped

2 medium roasted red bell peppers, cored and seeded

2 large red onions, chopped fine

3 cloves garlic, minced

2 teaspoons olive oil

1 tablespoon dried parsley

1 tablespoon dried basil

1 tablespoon lemon juice

Water as needed

Salt and pepper, to taste

- Preheat the oven to 400°F
- Place the tomatoes, pepper, and onions, along with the garlic, still in its skin, on a large cookie sheet. Drizzle with oil. Roast in the oven at 400°F for 45 to 50 minutes, or until the vegetables are browned and any liquid has evaporated. I recommend you turn the vegetables every 20 minutes or so, to ensure that they roast evenly.
- Remove from the oven and cool. When the vegetables are cool, place them in a blender along with the parsley, basil, and lemon juice, and puree. You will need to do this in batches, and you may need to add a small amount of water to the mixture, if it is too thick. Continue this process until all of the vegetables are pureed. Add the salt and pepper, and serve.

nutritional analysis per serving
37.39 calories; 73 g fat (27% calories from fat);
0.80 g protein; 4.32 g carbohydrate; 0 mg cholesterol;
76.13 mg sodium

Rory's Guacamole

PREP TIME: 10 minutes
SERVE: Serves 4

My son got inspired to create this recipe while vacationing in Arizona. It is a wonderful appetizer, and can be made in minutes if friends drop by or you are looking for a healthy snack. Avocadoes are a great source of heart healthy fats, and can be served with rice and beans, burritos, tacos, and many other dishes. A great garnish to many recipes.

2 avocados, peeled and mashed

1 large tomato, diced

½ cup diced red bell pepper

¾ cup finely chopped red onion

2 tablespoons lime juice, fresh if possible

2 jalapeño chile peppers, seeded and minced

1 clove garlic, minced

¼ cup chopped cilantro

Pinch of ground cumin

Salt and pepper, to taste

■ In a large bowl, combine all ingredients and mix together well.

nutritional analysis per serving
174.14 calories; 13.60 g fat (65% calories from fat); 2.54 g protein; 14.29 g carbohydrate; 0 mg cholesterol; 2.54 mg sodium

Spicy Walnuts

NO DAIRY OR EGGS

PREP TIME: 10 minutes
SERVE: Serves 16

Roasted nuts are very popular in salads. If you want to make these sweeter, replace the brown rice syrup with organic honey, and add enough to coat the nuts before baking. Honey is higher in carbohydrates but it adds a lovely shine and flavor to the nuts. You can explore other seasonings, too, such as curry, cloves, cinnamon, or black pepper. Be creative.

½ pound shelled walnuts
½ teaspoon garam masala
¼ teaspoon salt
½ teaspoon ground black pepper
1 teaspoon olive oil
1 teaspoon brown rice syrup

■ Preheat the oven to 300°F. Combine the walnuts, garam masala, salt, and pepper in a mixing bowl and stir well. Drizzle the oil and brown rice syrup evenly over the nuts. Toss well to coat, and place on a cookie sheet in a single layer. Bake in the oven for 7 minutes, or until toasted.

These nuts will store well in a sealed container for several days. You can use other nuts, such as pecans or almonds.

nutritional analysis per serving
198.02 calories; 19.07 g fat (81% calories from fat);
4.41 g protein; 5.98 g carbohydrate; 0 mg cholesterol;
38.98 mg sodium

soups, stews, and casseroles

Black Bean Soup

NO DAIRY, EGGS, OR NUTS

PREP TIME: 10 minutes to prepare, up to 2 hours to cook
SERVE: Serves 6

This is a great soup to make on a Sunday and then savor throughout the week. It's hearty, and full of protein and complex carbohydrates. If you prefer to use fresh beans, be sure to soak them overnight and then drain off the water and rinse before adding to the soup.

2 tablespoons olive oil

2 medium-size red onions, chopped

1 small red bell pepper, chopped

½ small green pepper, chopped

2 tablespoons minced fresh ginger

4 cloves garlic, minced

1 jalapeño chile pepper, seeded and minced

¼ teaspoon ground allspice

½ teaspoon thyme

2 (14½-ounce) cans black beans

8 cups water

2 medium-size sweet potatoes, peeled and cut into 1" cubes

1 tablespoon fruit sweetener or agave nectar

1 teaspoon salt

1 cup chopped cilantro

Black pepper

■ In a large pot or Dutch oven, heat the oil over medium heat. Add the onions and sauté 4 to 5 minutes. Add the peppers, yams, ginger, garlic, jalapeño pepper, allspice, and thyme. Cook 3 minutes. Add the beans and the water. Heat to boiling. Reduce the heat and simmer for 30 to 45 minutes, or until the veggies are tender. Add the fruit sweetener and salt. Place 1 cup of the soup in a blender and puree. Add it to the soup and stir. Add the cilantro and lots of black pepper.

> This recipe calls for fruit sweetener, but it is such a small amount that you really can do without it. You can also reduce the amount of water for a thicker soup, or substitute vegetable broth for additional nutrients.

nutritional analysis per serving
205.06 calories; 2.75 g fat (12% calories from fat); 6.68 g protein; 39.91 g carbohydrate; 0 mg cholesterol; 714.29 mg sodium

Borscht

PREP TIME: 1 hour
SERVE: Serves 6

Beets are abundant *in the summer months, making this a perfect soup for a sunny summer or fall supper. If you don't have a garden, visit your local farmers' market and you're sure to find all the necessary ingredients there.*

4 large beets with greens
1 tablespoon olive oil
2 medium-size carrots, chopped
2 large onions, chopped
1 pound tomatoes, crushed
4 cups vegetable broth
1 tablespoon lemon juice
1 tablespoon balsamic vinegar
1 tablespoon fresh dill
½ teaspoon salt
Dash of pepper

- Wash the beets and cut off the greens. Chop the greens and set aside. Without peeling, slice the beets. Steam or boil the beets for 20 to 30 minutes, or until done. Cool. Take the skins off the beets and cut the flesh into cubes. Set aside.
- In a Dutch oven or pot, heat the oil over medium heat and sauté the carrots and onions until the onion is soft, 4 to 5 minutes. Add the beet greens and cook until they are wilted. Add the tomatoes and cover. Simmer for 5 minutes, or until the tomatoes are cooked. Add the vegetable broth and simmer, covered, for 20 minutes, or until all the vegetables are tender. Add the beets, lemon juice, vinegar, dill, salt, and pepper. Heat through. Serve warm or cold.

nutritional analysis per serving
209.49 calories; 4.82 g fat (17% calories from fat); 6.33 g protein; 40.44 g carbohydrate; 0 mg cholesterol; 581.16 mg sodium

Brudet (Fish Stew)

NO DAIRY, EGGS, OR NUTS

PREP TIME: 1 hour
SERVE: Serves: 6

This is another family recipe. My grandparents came from the Czech Republic, and this soup was a family tradition passed through the generations. I grew up dipping bread into this soup, but it's great by itself.

1 large onion, chopped

1 stalk celery, chopped finely

1 large green bell pepper, chopped

3 cloves garlic, minced

¼ cup olive oil

1 (15-ounce) can tomato sauce

1 (15-ounce) can chopped tomatoes

15 ounces (1 can) water

Pinch of salt

½ teaspoon ground black pepper

½ teaspoon chile powder

2 hot red peppers, chopped finely

1 tablespoon chopped parsley

½ cup vinegar

½ cup red wine

1½ pounds salmon or other fish, skin and bones removed

- In a large pot, sauté the onion, celery, green bell pepper, and garlic in oil. Add the tomato sauce, chopped tomatoes, and water. Simmer for 30 minutes. Add the spices and herbs, vinegar, and wine. Add the fish and continue to cook until the fish is flaky (approximately 30 minutes).

nutritional analysis per serving
389.54 calories; 25.15 g fat (57% calories from fat); 26.88 g protein; 15.09 g carbohydrate; 51.03 mg cholesterol; 135.41 mg sodium

Carrot and Bean Soup

PREP TIME: 15 minutes to prepare and 30 minutes to cook
SERVE: Serves 8

This soup is full of antioxidants and great flavor. If you don't have a leek in the house, add more onion or a few stalks of celery.

5 cloves garlic, minced

1 tablespoon olive oil

1 large onion, chopped

1 large leek, chopped

1 quart chicken broth

2 pounds carrots, peeled and cut into chunks

1 teaspoon dried rosemary

1 teaspoon dried thyme

2 fresh sage leaves

30 ounces cannellini beans

½ cup dry sherry

½ teaspoon freshly ground pepper

Salt, to taste

- Preheat the oven to 400°F.
- Roast the garlic in its skin on a cookie sheet in the oven at 400°F for 20 minutes, or until soft. Peel and set aside. In a large Dutch oven or stockpot, heat the olive oil over medium heat, and add the onion and leek. Sauté until soft, about 5 minutes. Add the chicken broth, roasted garlic, and carrots. Bring to a boil. Reduce the heat and add the herbs. Simmer over medium-low heat until the carrots are tender, about 30 minutes. In batches, puree the soup mixture in a blender until smooth. Return to the soup pot and add the beans and sherry. Heat through. Season to taste with pepper and salt.

nutritional analysis per serving
256.49 calories; 3.34 g fat (11% calories from fat); 13.45 g protein; 41.27 g carbohydrate; 0 mg cholesterol; 473.22 mg sodium

Curried Ginger and Carrot Soup

NO DAIRY, EGGS, OR NUTS

PREP TIME: 15 minutes to prepare and 30 minutes to cook
SERVE: Serves 6

This soup will warm you clear to the bone. It is very hearty and served with a salad makes for a complete meal, either lunch or dinner.

2 tablespoons olive oil

1 medium-size onion, chopped finely

4 cloves garlic, minced

2 tablespoons peeled and minced fresh ginger

1 stalk fresh lemongrass, mashed (see box)

1 tablespoon curry powder

¼ teaspoon cayenne pepper

2 pounds carrots, peeled and sliced thinly

4 cups vegetable broth

4 cups water

1 cup light coconut milk

Salt

Pepper

2 tablespoons fresh cilantro

- In a large Dutch oven or stockpot, sauté the onion, garlic, fresh ginger, and mashed lemongrass over medium heat until soft, about 5 minutes. Add the curry powder, cayenne pepper, and carrots. Add the vegetable broth and water, and simmer for about 20 minutes, or until the carrots are tender. Add the coconut milk and simmer for 5 minutes longer. Remove the lemongrass from the soup and discard.

- In a blender or food processor, blend batches of the soup until smooth. When all of the soup has been pureed, return to the stockpot and adjust seasonings as desired. Garnish with fresh cilantro.

> Smash the end of the lemongrass with a heavy wooden spoon. Discard the top.

nutritional analysis per serving
243.12 calories; 13.73 g fat (46% of calories from fat); 4.45 g protein; 30.69 g carbohydrate; 0 mg cholesterol; 214.94 mg sodium

Curried Squash Soup

NO DAIRY, EGGS, OR PEANUTS

PREP TIME: 45 to 50 minutes
SERVE: Serves 6

This soup is very versatile. You can use different squashes, such as acorn or butternut squash. This soup keeps well in the refrigerator and can also be frozen. If you want more protein, add some tofu, or 2 cups of cooked organic chicken.

3 cups chopped yams

1 tablespoon olive oil

1 large onion, chopped

5 cloves garlic, chopped

2 tablespoons garam masala

½ teaspoon chile powder

1 quart vegetable stock

1 (14½-ounce) can diced tomatoes

½ cup almond butter

1 (14-ounce) can light coconut milk

¼ cup lime juice

¼ teaspoon cilantro

■ Heat a large Dutch oven and heat the oil. Sauté the onion until soft, about 5 minutes. Add the garlic, garam masala, and chile powder. Stir well and continue cooking for 1 to 2 minutes. Add the yams, and sauté for another 3 minutes. Add the vegetable stock and the tomatoes. Bring to a boil, then reduce the heat to medium low and simmer for 20 minutes, or until the yams are soft. While the soup is cooking, combine the almond butter with the coconut milk. Add it to the soup slowly, stirring to blend. Heat the soup through, then blend in batches until all of the soup has been pureed. When all of the soup is blended, return it to the Dutch oven and add the lime juice. Serve with the cilantro, if desired.

nutritional analysis per serving
277.09 calories; 18.90 g fat (57% of calories from fat); 5.06 g protein; 25.95 g carbohydrate; 0 mg cholesterol; 400.05 mg sodium

Egg Drop Soup

PREP TIME: 10 minutes to prepare and 15 minutes to cook
SERVE: Serves 4

This quick, easy soup is full of protein. If you want to make homemade chicken stock, which is always my preference, you will find a recipe on page 60. Homemade stock always adds so much flavor to a soup.

2 cloves garlic, minced

6 ounces snow peas, cut in bite-size pieces

1–2 teaspoon peeled and minced fresh ginger

4 cups organic low-sodium chicken broth

3 cups water

½ cup mushrooms, sliced

4 teaspoons wheat-free tamari sauce

3 large eggs, beaten

Dash of sesame oil and rice wine vinegar

3 green onions, sliced

- In a small skillet, sauté the garlic, snow peas, and ginger for 1 to 2 minutes. Heat the chicken broth and water until it comes to a boil. Add the garlic mixture and mushrooms. Cook over medium heat for 2 to 3 minutes. Add the tamari sauce. Increase the heat to high.

- Stirring constantly, add the beaten eggs, one at a time. The eggs will feather out into the soup. Reduce heat and season with the sesame oil and rice wine vinegar. Top each bowl with sliced green onions.

nutritional analysis per serving

116.93 calories; 5.35 g fat (30% of calories from fat); 11.75 g protein; 7.07 g carbohydrate; 158.63 mg cholesterol; 540.82 mg sodium

Fruit and Berry Soup

PREP TIME: 15 minutes to prepare and 2 hours to chill
SERVE: Serves 4

Another summer favorite. With so many fruits and berries available in the summer, don't let this recipe stunt your creativity; try substituting other fruits. Cold soups are often a hit with the kids, so give it a whirl.

1 peach, peeled, pitted, and diced

1 nectarine, pitted and diced

1 cantaloupe or honeydew, peeled, seeded, and diced

1 cup water or apple juice

1 lemon, squeezed

Blueberries or strawberries

Peppermint or spearmint sprigs

- In a large stockpot, combine the fruit and water. Cook, covered, over medium heat for 10 to 12 minutes.
- Remove from the heat and place in a blender or food processor. Puree until smooth. Add the lemon juice and pour into a large bowl.
- Chill thoroughly, about 2 hours. Serve garnished with fresh berries and mint leaves.

nutritional analysis per serving
76.77 calories; .35 g fat (4% of calories from fat); 1.11 g protein; 19.18 g carbohydrate; 0 mg cholesterol; 6.27 mg sodium

Homemade Chicken Broth

PREP TIME: 10 minutes to prepare and 2 to 3 hours to cook
SERVE: Makes 3 quarts

This is a great base for many of the recipes in this book. I like to freeze this broth so I always have it on hand when I need it. When you thaw it out, be sure to scoop out any remaining fat that will rise to the top of the container.

3 pounds bony chicken pieces

2 stalks celery, cut into chunks

2 medium-size carrots, cut into chunks

2 medium-size onions, quartered

2 bay leaves

½ teaspoon dried rosemary, crushed

½ teaspoon dried thyme

8–10 whole peppercorns

4 quarts cold water

■ Mix all of the ingredients in a large stockpot. Bring to a boil. Skim off the foam as it rises, and then lower the heat. Simmer for 2 to 3 hours. Strain the broth through a sieve, discarding the solids, and place in a lidded container. Use immediately, or save for later. Be sure to cool completely before freezing, to enable you to skim off the fat before storing.

nutritional analysis per serving
130.42 calories; 4.73 g fat (33% calories from fat); 16.03 g protein; 5.33 g carbohydrate; 45.83 mg cholesterol; 98.68 mg sodium

Homemade Vegetable Stock

PREP TIME: 15 minutes to prepare and 2 to 3 hours to cook
SERVE: Serves 6

I use vegetable stock in many of my recipes. It's so nutritious, and adds such a lovely flavor. This is a basic soup stock recipe, but you can add any vegetables you want to it. Do you have some vegetables in the bin that need to be used up? Throw them in this stock and they won't go to waste. This stock will store in the refrigerator for up to a week. You can also freeze for up to two months.

1 tablespoon olive oil
2 large onions, chopped
2 stalks celery, chopped
2 large carrots, chopped
1 large red potato, chopped
2 cups mushrooms, sliced
6 cloves garlic
½ pound spinach
2 large tomatoes, chopped
1 tablespoon dried parsley
8 whole peppercorns
3 quarts water

■ Wash and trim all vegetables. Heat the oil in a large pot and sauté the onion, celery, carrots, potato, and mushrooms for 3 to 4 minutes. Add the garlic and spinach, and continue cooking for 1 minute. Add the tomatoes, parsley, peppercorns, and water. Bring to a boil, then reduce heat and simmer for 2 to 3 hours, or until the liquid has been reduced by half. Strain the broth through a sieve, discarding the solids, and place in a lidded container. Use immediately, or save for later. Be sure to cool completely before freezing.

nutritional analysis per serving
107.98 calories; 2.81 g fat (23% calories from fat);
4.07 g protein; 19.24 g carbohydrate; 0 mg cholesterol;
90.64 mg sodium

Jeff's Vegetable Soup

NO DAIRY, EGGS, OR NUTS

PREP TIME: 1½ hours
SERVE: Serves 6

My son Jeff doesn't remember creating this soup, as he was only about four years old, but I wrote it down, and I want to share it with you. To add some protein to the soup, add some chicken, bison, or tofu.

4 cloves garlic, minced

1 large onion, chopped

4 large stalks celery, chopped

1 small red bell pepper, chopped

3 small carrots, chopped

½ pound mushrooms, stems removed

1 cup cabbage, coarsely chopped

1 large zucchini, chopped

½ bunch broccoli, chopped

1 tablespoons olive oil

½ cup tomato sauce

1 pound fresh or 1 (16-ounce) can tomatoes

4 cups vegetable broth

4 cups water

3 bay leaves

1 teaspoon fresh basil

1 teaspoon dried thyme

½ teaspoon freshly ground pepper

½ cup red wine (optional)

■ In a large stockpot, sauté the vegetables in oil for 4 to 5 minutes. Add the tomato sauce, tomatoes, vegetable broth, water, bay leaves, and herbs. Add the wine if desired. Simmer for 1½ hours, or until the vegetables are tender.

> To make a heartier soup, add brown rice or beans. Serve warm.

nutritional analysis per serving
118.19 calories; 1.26 g fat (5% calories from fat);
5.28 g protein; 25.53 g carbohydrate; 0 mg cholesterol;
175.73 mg sodium

Lentil Soup with Veggies

NO DAIRY, EGGS, OR NUTS

PREP TIME: 10 minutes to prepare, 50 minutes to cook
SERVE: Serves 4

My grandma was big on lentil soup, so this is my version of her basic lentil soup. I added the spinach and squash. She always included celery in her recipe, so you may want to add a few stalks next time you make it.

- 1 tablespoon olive oil
- 1 large onion, chopped
- ½ large red bell pepper, chopped
- 1 cup butternut squash, peeled and cubed
- 2 small carrots, chopped
- 3 cloves garlic, chopped finely
- 1 small tomato, chopped
- 1 cup red lentils
- 6 cups vegetable broth or water
- 1 bunch spinach, washed and chopped
- 1 tablespoon balsamic vinegar
- ¼ teaspoon thyme, ground
- 1½ teaspoons salt
- ½ teaspoon pepper

- Heat the oil in a Dutch oven or stockpot over medium heat. Add the onion, bell pepper, squash, carrots, and garlic; sauté until tender, stirring frequently. Add the tomato, lentils, and vegetable broth. Bring to a boil, then lower the heat and simmer for about 45 minutes, or until the lentils are soft.
- When the lentils are done, add the spinach, balsamic vinegar, ground thyme, salt, and pepper, and cook until the spinach is wilted and the soup is heated through.

nutritional analysis per serving
282.74 calories; 5.75 g fat (18% calories from fat); 13.27 g protein; 47.00 g carbohydrate; 1.64 mg cholesterol; 1124.43 mg sodium

Mediterranean Stew

PREP/COOK TIME: 30 to 40 minutes
SERVE: Serves 6

When a large crowd is coming for dinner, this is what I make. Everyone loves it and it feeds several, especially if you serve it over polenta, quinoa, spaghetti squash, or rice.

¼ cup extra-virgin olive oil

2 large onions, chopped

2 cloves garlic, chopped finely

½ teaspoon cayenne pepper

1 teaspoon ground cinnamon

1 teaspoon ground turmeric

1 teaspoon ground cumin

½ teaspoon paprika

1 cup carrots, sliced

1 cup yams, peeled and chopped

4 cups butternut or other winter squash, peeled and cubed

1 large red bell pepper, sliced

3 cups eggplant, cubed

2 cups mushrooms, stemmed and halved

½ cup currants

1½ cups cooked garbanzo beans (save the liquid)

¼ cup chopped fresh parsley

- Heat a Dutch oven over medium heat and heat the olive oil. Sauté the onions for 3 to 5 minutes, then add the garlic and cook for 1 minute. Add all the spices and cook for 1 minute more.
- Add the carrots and sauté until the color deepens. Add the yam and squash, and sauté for 2 to 3 minutes. Continue this process, adding the pepper, eggplant, and mushrooms until you have sautéed them all. If the stew is dry, add some of the garbanzo bean liquid. If there is juice from the veggies in the pot, don't add more liquid. Cook until the vegetables are soft.
- Add the garbanzo beans, currants, and parsley. Serve over polenta.

nutritional analysis per serving
290.19 calories; 10.41 g fat (31% calories from fat); 7.55 g protein; 48.16 g carbohydrate; 0 mg cholesterol; 158.94 mg sodium

Mulligatawny Soup

PREP/COOK TIME: 30 to 40 minutes
SERVE: Serves 4

The idea behind *this soup is to include everything in the vegetable bin. It makes a great lazy Sunday afternoon meal.*

1 small onion, chopped finely

1 stalk celery, chopped

2 medium-size carrots, sliced

1 medium-size zucchini, chopped

1 large apple, chopped

3 tablespoons olive oil

1 tablespoon tapioca flour

¼ teaspoon dried thyme

1 tablespoon curry powder

4 cups low-sodium chicken broth

1 bay leaf

1 teaspoon lemon zest

1 cup diced cooked chicken

½ cup soy milk

½ teaspoon freshly ground pepper

Salt, if desired

- In a large stockpot, sauté the veggies and apple in the olive oil for 8 to 10 minutes, or until tender. Stir in the tapioca flour, thyme, and curry powder. Cook for 1 to 2 minutes.
- Add the chicken broth, bay leaf, and lemon zest, and simmer for another 12 to 15 minutes. Add the cooked chicken, soy milk, and freshly ground pepper. Heat through. Season with salt if desired.

nutritional analysis per serving

245.0 calories; 13.33 g fat (43% calories from fat); 9.20 g protein; 26.22 g carbohydrate; 0 mg cholesterol; 324.92 mg sodium

Mung Bean Soup

NO DAIRY, EGGS, OR NUTS

PREP/COOK TIME: 60 to 70 minutes
SERVE: Serves 4

I made this soup for my cooking class and they loved it. They fought over who got to take home the leftovers. I like this soup for dinner, and then lunch the next day, and hopefully, the day after that.

1 cup dried mung beans, washed

2 cups water

1 large onion, chopped finely

1 tablespoon olive oil

2 medium-size carrots, diced

2 tablespoons peeled and minced fresh ginger

1 stalk celery, diced

4 cloves garlic

2 medium-size tomatoes, chopped

½ teaspoon ground turmeric

1 teaspoon curry powder

1 teaspoon ground cumin

3 cups vegetable stock

1 cup light coconut milk

Juice of 1 large lime

½ cup chopped fresh cilantro

- Place the beans in a soup pot. Cover with water and bring to a boil. Reduce the heat and simmer until the beans are soft, 35 to 40 minutes.

- In a large pot, sauté the onion in the oil until soft, about 5 minutes. Add the carrot, ginger, and celery, and continue to cook for another 4 to 5 minutes. Add the garlic and tomatoes, and sauté for another minute. Combine all the spices in a small bowl and add to the vegetable mixture. Add the beans, water, and vegetable stock. Simmer for 15 to 20 minutes or until the vegetables are tender. Add the coconut milk, lime juice, and cilantro and heat through. Season with salt and pepper.

nutritional analysis per serving
142.59 calories; 5.54 g fat (30% calories from fat);
3.66 g protein; 22.77 g carbohydrate; 0 mg cholesterol;
240.10 mg sodium

Pumpkin Soup

NO DAIRY, EGGS, OR NUTS

PREP TIME: 10 minutes to prepare and 25 minutes to cook
SERVE: Serves 8

In the fall when the pumpkins are abundant, this soup is even better made with fresh pumpkin. You would want to substitute about 3½ cups of fresh pumpkin for the canned pumpkin. The coconut milk really makes this soup smooth. The fresh ginger will warm you through and through.

2 tablespoons olive oil

½ cup red onion, chopped fine

2 cloves garlic, minced

2 cooking apples, peeled and diced

½ teaspoon cumin

2 teaspoon peeled and minced fresh ginger

1 teaspoon curry powder

1 (30-ounce) can pureed pumpkin

1 (28-ounce) can chicken broth

1 cup coconut milk

Dash of salt

¼ teaspoon crushed red pepper flakes

■ In a large stockpot, heat the oil over medium heat. Add the onion and apples. Sauté until soft, about 3 minutes. Add the garlic and cook for 1 minute.

■ In a small bowl, mix together the cumin, ginger, and curry powder. Add to the apple mixture and cook for 1 to 2 minutes. Add the pumpkin and chicken broth. Bring to a boil, then lower the heat and simmer for 10 minutes. Let cool.

■ Puree in a blender or food processor in small batches until all of the soup is smooth, then return to the stockpot. Add the coconut milk, salt, and pepper, and heat through.

nutritional analysis per serving
134.29 calories; 7.10 g fat (45% calories from fat);
4.29 g protein; 16.12 g carbohydrate; 0 mg cholesterol;
621.04 mg sodium

Roasted Butternut Squash Soup

NO DAIRY, EGGS, OR NUTS

PREP TIME: 20 minutes to prepare and about 1 hour to cook
SERVE: Serves 4

Where was butternut squash when I was growing up? All we had was zucchini squash and, boiled, it left little to be desired. Butternut squash, on the other hand, is firm, full of flavor, and good for you. I think you will really enjoy this soup.

1 large butternut squash (1½ pounds)

Vegetable oil spray

2 tablespoons olive oil

4 large apples

1½ cups onions, chopped fine

2 large shallots, minced

½ teaspoon dried rosemary

1 teaspoon dried thyme

4 cups chicken broth

½ cup light coconut milk or soy milk

¼ teaspoon freshly ground pepper

■ Slice the butternut squash and scoop out all the seeds. Preheat the oven to 400°F. Spray the bottom of a baking sheet with vegetable oil spray. Lightly coat the inside of the squash with oil. Place the squash cut side down on the baking sheet. Bake in the oven for 35 to 40 minutes, or until the squash is tender. Remove from the oven and cool. After the squash cools, scoop out the insides, cut into chunks, and set aside in a medium-size bowl.

■ Wash, peel, and dice the apples. Set aside.

■ In a large Dutch oven or stockpot, combine the onion and shallots, and sauté for 4 to 5 minutes, or until soft. Add the diced apple and cooled squash and continue to cook for 6 to 8 minutes. Add the rosemary, thyme, and chicken broth. Simmer for about 10 minutes. Place the soup in batches in a blender or food processor. Blend until smooth and return each batch to the Dutch oven or stockpot. Add more chicken broth or water if the soup is too thick. When you have pureed all of the soup, add the coconut milk and freshly ground pepper, and heat through.

nutritional analysis per serving
275.46 calories; 9.09 g fat (29% calories from fat); 7.60 g protein; 45.42 g carbohydrate; 0 mg cholesterol; 775.63 mg sodium

Salmon Chowder

PREP/COOK TIME: 45 to 50 minutes
SERVE: Serves 6

In the Pacific Northwest, we have an abundance of salmon. This is a great soup to make when you have some leftover salmon, or you want a special treat. It calls for heavy cream, but I prefer milk. I don't think soy milk will work in this recipe; I worry the flavor will overpower the delicate flavor of the salmon, but if you are daring, give it a try.

3 tablespoons olive oil

2 small onions, chopped

1 large potato, chopped

2 cups chicken broth

3 cups water

3 cups cream or milk

1 tablespoon chives

1 pound salmon, cooked

1 cup white corn

½ teaspoon pepper

- In a large stockpot or Dutch oven, heat the olive oil over medium heat. Add the onions and sauté until soft, 4 to 5 minutes. Add the potato and continue cooking another 10 minutes. Add the chicken broth and water, and simmer over low heat for 15 minutes or until potatoes are tender.
- Add the milk, chives, salmon, corn, and pepper, and heat through.

nutritional analysis per serving
295.42 calories; 14.77 g fat (44% calories from fat); 21.17 g protein; 19.97 g carbohydrate; 29.59 mg cholesterol; 1758 mg sodium

Sweet Potato Soup

NO DAIRY, EGGS, OR NUTS

PREP/COOK TIME: 20 to 30 minutes
SERVE: Serves 2

Have a baked sweet potato in the refrigerator? Make this simple soup and you have a meal. It doesn't make enough for a family, so if you need to feed more than two, double the recipe.

1 cup peeled sweet potato, cooked

1½ cups low-sodium chicken stock

¾ cup soy milk

Salt and pepper, to taste

Grated nutmeg, if desired

■ Combine the sweet potato, chicken stock, and soy milk in a food processor or blender. Puree until smooth. Heat through and season to taste with salt and pepper (and nutmeg, if desired).

nutritional analysis per serving
125.03 calories; 2.98 g fat (20% of calories from fat); 8.12 g protein; 18.30 g carbohydrate; 0 mg cholesterol; 73.79 mg sodium

Tomato and Corn Soup

PREP/COOK TIME: 40 minutes
SERVE: Serves 4

This soup is so good made with fresh tomatoes and corn. If you have an herb garden that grows cilantro and basil, you have all you need. You can also replace the cilantro and basil with oregano or rosemary, and add some chopped zucchini.

1 tablespoon oil

1 onion, chopped

1 clove garlic, minced

1 stalk celery, chopped

2 cups corn

1 (24-ounce) can tomatoes, crushed

4 cups vegetable or chicken stock

½ teaspoon salt

½ teaspoon pepper

½ cup chopped fresh cilantro

■ In a large cooking pot or Dutch oven, sauté the onion, garlic, and celery in the oil. Add the corn, crushed tomatoes, vegetable stock, salt, and pepper. Bring to the boil, then reduce the heat and simmer for about 30 minutes. Puree in a blender. Add the cilantro and heat through.

nutritional analysis per serving
319.67 calories; 8.16 g fat (23% of calories from fat); 10.50 g protein; 56.57 g carbohydrate; 2.46 mg cholesterol; 1651.19 mg sodium

Turkey Stock

PREP TIME: 10 minutes to prepare and 2 hours to cook
SERVE: Makes 3 cups

Have some leftover turkey in the fridge? Toss it in the pot, cover with water, add the vegetables listed here, and you will have a great turkey stock in no time. Freeze this stock for use in soups and stews at a later date.

2 tablespoons olive oil

1 large onion, chopped

1 large stalk celery, chopped

1½ pound turkey parts

2 large carrots, chopped

9 cups water

10 large whole peppercorns

■ In a large Dutch oven, heat the oil over medium-high heat. Add all the ingredients except the water and peppercorns, and sauté for about 20 minutes, until the veggies are dark brown. Add the water and peppercorns, and bring to a boil. Reduce the heat and simmer for about 1 to 2 hours, or until the stock is reduced to 3 cups.

■ Remove all the turkey parts and strain the broth. Spoon off the fat and store the stock in the refrigerator until needed or freeze.

nutritional analysis per serving
114.82 calories; 7.51 g fat (58% of calories from fat); 4.19 g protein; 8.40 g carbohydrate; 11.93 mg cholesterol; 75.14 mg sodium

White Bean Stew

NO DAIRY, EGGS, OR NUTS

PREP/COOK TIME: 30 minutes
SERVE: Serves 6

Look at the protein content in this stew. It is amazing. It tastes great, provides complex carbohydrates and protein and a dose of fat, so you have a complete meal here. Just add a salad and you have dinner. Hopefully, you'll have leftovers for lunch tomorrow.

1 large yellow bell pepper

1 large red bell pepper

4 cloves garlic, roasted

2 tablespoons olive oil

1 large onion, sliced

½ small zucchini, sliced thinly

¼ cup white wine

2 cups vegetable or chicken broth

1 (28-ounce) can cannellini beans, washed and drained

2 tablespoons chopped parsley

½ teaspoon dried rosemary

1 tablespoon balsamic vinegar

½ teaspoon freshly ground pepper

- Preheat the oven to 400°F.
- Spray cookie sheet lightly with vegetable oil. Place the peppers and garlic on a cookie sheet and roast them in the oven at 400°F for 20 minutes (be sure not to peel the garlic before roasting). Set aside.
- In a large stockpot or Dutch oven, heat the oil over medium heat and add the onion and zucchini. Sauté for about 4 minutes, or until soft. Add the wine and simmer until the liquid evaporates, about 5 minutes. Next, add the vegetable broth and bring to a boil. Add the beans, parsley, and rosemary, reduce the heat to medium-low, and simmer for 10 minutes. Slice the roasted peppers thinly, peel the garlic and cut it in half, and add to the soup along with the balsamic vinegar. Heat through. Garnish with the freshly ground pepper.

> This soup is very hearty and, combined with a salad, makes a great light supper.

nutritional analysis per serving
482.18 calories; 8.23 g fat (14% of calories of fat);
27.02 g protein; 77.45 g carbohydrate; 0 mg cholesterol;
82.18 mg sodium

Barb's Lamb and Zucchini Casserole

PREP TIME: 10 minutes to prepare and 35 to 40 minutes to bake
SERVE: Serves 8

This is a great dish to bring to a potluck. It serves several and everyone will love it. If you prefer a dairy-free version, just omit the cheese. It still tastes good.

1 tablespoon olive oil

1 pound ground lamb

¾ cup red onion, chopped finely

2 cloves garlic, minced

2 (10-ounce) packages frozen spinach, or 1 bunch fresh, chopped

½ teaspoon fresh basil, plus extra for garnish

¼ teaspoon grated nutmeg

⅔ cup water

1–2 teaspoons arrowroot

6 ounces mozzarella cheese, grated

2 small zucchini, sliced thinly

¼ cup Parmesan cheese

Salt and pepper, to taste

- Preheat the oven to 350°F.
- Heat a large skillet on medium heat and heat the oil. Brown the ground lamb with the chopped onion and garlic. Drain off any excess fat. Combine the drained spinach (squeeze out excess liquid), ½ teaspoon of basil, and nutmeg. Add to the meat mixture. Mix well and set aside.
- Combine the water and arrowroot, and mix to dissolve. Pour over the meat mixture.
- Place the meat mixture in an 11 × 7-inch baking dish. Sprinkle the mozzarella on top of the meat mixture. Arrange the zucchini on top and sprinkle with the Parmesan. Sprinkle on extra basil as desired. Season to taste with salt and pepper.
- Bake, covered, for 30 minutes at 350°F. Uncover and bake an additional 5 to 10 minutes, or until the casserole is bubbly and golden.

nutritional analysis per serving
250.30 calories; 17.50 g fat (61% calories from fat); 16.90 g protein; 7.9 g carbohydrate; 52.0 mg cholesterol; 246.10 mg sodium

Tamale Cheese Casserole

NO NUTS

PREP TIME: 45 to 50 minutes to prep and 50 minutes to bake
SERVE: Serves 10

This is my son Jeffrey's favorite dinner. It is very filling, but can be served with a salad and/or guacamole. It is wonderful the next day, if you have any leftovers!

1 tablespoon olive oil

1 cup onion, chopped

2 cloves garlic, minced

1 large red bell pepper, chopped finely

1 pound ground turkey, beef, or bison

1 cup tomato sauce, homemade if possible

1 (16-ounce) can whole tomatoes

1¼ cups (12 ounces) white corn, frozen or fresh

1 tablespoon chile powder

½ teaspoon salt

4 ounces olives

Vegetable oil spray

Crust:

¾ cup cornmeal

3 cups milk

2 large eggs, beaten

1 tablespoon butter or shortening

3 cups Cheddar cheese, grated

½ teaspoon salt

- In a large skillet, heat the oil and sauté the onion until soft, 4 to 5 minutes. Add the garlic and red bell pepper, and continue to sauté for 1 to 2 minutes longer. Remove the veggies from the skillet and set aside. Add the meat to the skillet and cook until it loses its red color, 5 to 6 minutes. Add the tomato sauce, whole tomatoes, corn, chile powder, veggies, and ½ teaspoon of salt. Cover the skillet and simmer on medium-low for 40 minutes. Add the olives and remove from heat. Set aside.

- For the crust, combine the cornmeal and 1 cup of the milk in a bowl. Set aside. Preheat oven to 350°F.

- Heat the other 2 cups of the milk in a saucepan with the butter and ½ teaspoon of salt. Heat to boiling. Slowly add the cornmeal mixture and stir constantly until it has thickened. Once it is thick, reduce the heat, cover, and simmer on low for 15 minutes. Add the eggs and 1 cup of the cheese. Remove from the heat, and stir to mix until the cheese has melted.

- Lightly spray a 9 × 11-inch baking pan with cooking spray and then sprinkle some of the cornmeal mixture on the bottom of the pan. Top with the meat mixture and then dollop more of the cornmeal mixture on top of the meat. Spread the remaining cheese on top and bake in the oven for 50 minutes, or until the mixture is bubbly and golden brown.

nutritional analysis per serving
462.8 calories; 22.10 g fat (42% of calories from fat); 22.30 g protein; 44.50 g carbohydrate; 103.00 mg cholesterol; 739.0 mg sodium

Wild Mushroom Casserole

PREP TIME: 15 minutes to prepare and 60 minutes to bake
SERVE: Serves 8

This is yummy. *Feel free to use whatever mushrooms are available, but the chanterelles really give this dish a wonderful flavor. This casserole makes great leftovers, as the flavors seem to deepen as it ages. Feel free to experiment with other cheeses in this recipe, such as Gorgonzola or Swiss.*

1 tablespoons olive oil

3 cups chanterelle mushrooms

4½ cups cremini mushrooms

½ cup onion, chopped

1 tablespoon chopped fresh parsley, or 1 teaspoon. dried

1 tablespoon torn or chopped fresh basil, or 1 teaspoon. dried

1 teaspoon dried oregano

½ teaspoon sea salt

½ teaspoon freshly ground pepper, plus extra, to taste

4 cups yams, sliced thinly

Vegetable oil spray

1 cup Monterey Jack cheese, grated

½ cup chicken or vegetable broth

■ In a large skillet, heat the oil and sauté the mushrooms until the juice begins to run and the mushrooms are soft, about 2 minutes. Add the onion and sauté for 2 to 3 minutes. Add the parsley, basil, oregano, salt, and ½ teaspoon of ground pepper. Heat for about 1 minute. Preheat oven to 400°F.

■ Now, lightly oil a 7 × 11-inch casserole dish and place in it a layer of yams, followed by a layer of mushrooms. Sprinkle some of the cheese on top, and then add another layer of yams. Continue this process until all of the yams and the mushroom mixture are used up, finishing with the cheese. Pour the chicken broth over the cheese and sprinkle with more freshly ground pepper, if desired. Cover and bake for 1 hour. Remove the cover and let stand at room temperature for 5 minutes before serving.

nutritional analysis per serving
164.57 calories; 5.36 g fat (29% of calories from fat); 6.68 g protein; 23.30 g carbohydrate; 14.59 mg cholesterol; 290.80 mg sodium

main
courses

Baba's Stuffed Zucchini

NO NUTS

PREP TIME: 20 minutes to prepare and 20 minutes to bake
SERVE: Serves 6

This recipe is named after my grand-mother. She always had an abundance of zucchini in the summer and early fall. She was an avid gardener and taught me how to make this recipe.

6 large zucchini

1 large red bell pepper, chopped

½ pound mushrooms, cleaned and stemmed

3 cloves garlic, chopped

3 tablespoons olive oil

1 teaspoon dried oregano

¼ cup chopped fresh parsley

½ cup grated Parmesan cheese

2 eggs, beaten

- Preheat the oven to 350°F.
- Wash the zucchini and place in a steamer. Steam until crisp-tender, about 10 minutes. Cut off the ends and cut the squash in half lengthwise. Scoop out the insides, mash, and place in a large bowl. Set the zucchini shells aside. In a large skillet, sauté the red bell pepper, mushrooms, and garlic in oil until soft, 5 to 7 minutes. Add the herbs, mashed zucchini pulp, and half the cheese mixture. Mix well. Add the beaten eggs and cook until the mixture is thick and heated through. Stuff into the zucchini shells and top with the remainder of the cheese. Place in a 9 × 11-inch baking dish. Bake until heated through and the cheese has melted, about 20 minutes. You can add other leftover vegetables to this mixture. Use up whatever you have in your refrigerator!

nutritional analysis per serving
196.52 calories; 11.84 g fat (53% calories from fat); 10 g protein; 14.57 g carbohydrate; 89.11 mg cholesterol; 247.28 mg sodium

Baked Salmon

NO DAIRY, EGGS, OR NUTS

PREP TIME: 15 minutes to prepare and about 35 minutes to bake
SERVE: Serves 4

This recipe is so easy to make, and provides a healthy dose of omega-3s. If you are concerned about the amount of fat, decrease the oil to 2 tablespoons. It will suffice. You can add other herbs, too, such as rosemary or my favorite, herbes de provence.

4 tablespoons olive oil
2 cloves garlic, chopped finely
1 small onion, chopped finely
2 tablespoons red wine
1 tablespoon minced fresh basil
Salt and pepper, to taste
1½ pounds salmon fillets
Lemon wedges, if desired

- Preheat the oven to 350°F.
- In a large skillet, heat the olive oil. Sauté the garlic and onion until soft, 4 to 5 minutes. Add the wine, basil, salt, and pepper. Cook for 5 minutes.
- Place the salmon in a large baking dish and pour the olive oil and vegetable mixture over the fish. Bake for about 35 minutes, or until done.
- Serve with lemon wedges, if desired. Can be accompanied by rice, fresh green beans, and a salad.

nutritional analysis per serving
374.34 calories; 24.35 g fat (5% calories from fat); 34.17 g protein; 3.39 g carbohydrate; 93.56 mg cholesterol; 76.49 mg sodium

Barbecued Country-Style Spareribs

PREP TIME: 20 minutes to prepare and up to 2 hours to bake
SERVE: Serves 4

If you prefer beef to pork, feel free to replace them in this recipe. I like to slice a large onion and spread it over the ribs before I add the sauce. Cooking the ribs slowly, with the sauce found on page 186 is the secret to the success of this recipe. You can also prepare this dish using a crock pot if you prefer, cooking on low for several hours.

1½–2 pounds pork spareribs
1 recipe Barbecue Sauce (page 186)

- Preheat the oven to 325°F.
- Boil the spareribs for 15 minutes to remove excess fat. Place in a roasting pan or Dutch oven and cover with barbecue sauce. Bake for 2 to 3 hours, or until the meat is very tender.

nutritional analysis per serving
324.32 calories: 26.76 g fat (74% calories from fat); 19.38 g protein; 0 g carbohydrate; 88.45 mg cholesterol; 86.18 mg sodium

Basil Chicken Curry

PREP/COOK TIME: 45 minutes
SERVE: Serves 4

This is one *of my favorite recipes in*
this book. It is so flavorful and feeds a
crowd or provides wonderful leftovers.
I serve it over red rice but you can
serve it over any rice, or polenta for
that matter. You will truly enjoy it. The
curry is mild, so it does not take over
the flavor of the dish.

½ teaspoon ground cardamom

½ teaspoon ground cinnamon

¼ teaspoon ground cloves

½ teaspoon ground coriander

½ teaspoon cumin

½ teaspoon salt and freshly
   ground pepper

¼ teaspoon ground turmeric

½ teaspoon chile powder

4 skinless, boneless chicken
   breasts, cut into bite-size
   pieces

1 tablespoon olive oil

1 large red onion, chopped

6 cloves garlic, minced

1 small red bell pepper, sliced

½ small zucchini, sliced

3 teaspoons arrowroot

1 (14-ounce) can light coconut
   milk

1 tablespoon peeled and finely
   chopped ginger

5 tablespoons snipped fresh
   basil

■ In a large bowl, stir together the cardamom,
cinnamon, cloves, coriander, cumin, salt, pepper, turmeric, and chile powder. Wash the
chicken breasts and dry on a paper towel. Add
the chicken to the spices and set aside for 20
to 30 minutes. You can also cover the chicken
and leave it in the refrigerator for several hours
or overnight if preferred.

■ Heat the oil in a large skillet and sauté the
onion, garlic, red bell pepper, and zucchini
over medium-high heat for 4 to 5 minutes.
Remove the vegetables from the skillet and
set aside in a small bowl.

■ Add the chicken breasts to the oil and sauté
until the chicken is tender and cooked
through. Add more oil if needed. Remove
the chicken from the skillet and add to the
vegetables. In the meantime, combine the
arrowroot and light coconut milk and stir
until well blended.

■ Over medium-high heat add the arrowroot
and coconut milk to the skillet and cook until
the mixture has become bubbly and thickened. Add the ginger, basil, chicken, and vegetables and heat through.

■ Garnish with fresh basil and serve over
brown or red rice.

nutritional analysis per serving
418.29 calories; 13.91 g fat (29% calories from fat);
56.32 g protein; 13.16 g carbohydrate; 136.88 mg cholesterol; 419.21 mg sodium

Beef and Broccoli

PREP/COOK TIME: 45 minutes
SERVE: Serves 4

Flank steak is tough by nature, so it's important to cut it as thinly as you can. If you wish to use another oil, grapeseed oil, with all of its wonderful attributes, is a perfect substitute. It leaves no aftertaste, doesn't affect the flavor of the foods cooked in it, and can withstand high heat. Grapeseed oil is also very high in linoleic acid, which is good for the heart.

½ pound flank steak

1 tablespoon arrowroot

1 teaspoon sesame oil

2 tablespoons tamari sauce

1 pound broccoli

1 large red bell pepper, diced very finely

1 large red onion, chopped finely

2 cloves garlic, minced

3 tablespoons peanut oil

Water as needed

- Place the meat in the freezer for half an hour to make it easier to cut. Take it out and slice it into diagonal strips. Cut again into very thin pieces and set aside.
- Place the arrowroot, sesame oil, and tamari sauce in a shallow bowl and add the meat. Marinate for 30 minutes.
- Prepare the broccoli, red bell pepper, onion, and garlic for sautéing: Cut the florets from the broccoli, then remove the fibrous outer layer from the stalk and slice the rest.
- Heat 2 tablespoons of the peanut oil in a large skillet and add the meat. Sauté the flank steak in the peanut oil for about 2 minutes. Remove from the heat and set aside.
- Heat another tablespoon of the oil until it is almost smoking. Add the broccoli and onion and stir-fry for about 3 minutes. Add the garlic and red bell pepper, and continue stir-frying for 2 minutes more. Add a small amount of water. Cover and steam the vegetables for 2 to 3 minutes. Vegetables should be bright in color, and crisp-tender.
- Add the marinade (arrowroot, sesame oil, and tamari sauce) to the mixture and heat until it thickens. Serve over rice.

nutritional analysis per serving
244.09 calories; 15.78 g fat (57% calories from fat); 16.60 g protein; 11.23 g carbohydrate; 19.85 mg cholesterol; 563.30 mg sodium

Beef Stir-Fry

NO DAIRY, EGGS, OR NUTS

PREP/COOK TIME: 45 minutes
SERVE: Serves 6

This recipe is quite filling, and can be modified as you wish. You can replace the veggie broth with beef broth, or you can substitute chicken for the beef and use chicken stock.

3 tablespoons Asian fish sauce
½ cup unsweetened ketchup
1 tablespoon agave nectar
1 tablespoon lime juice
1 (12-ounce) boneless sirloin steak, cut into strips
1½ teaspoons arrowroot
½ cup vegetable broth
2 teaspoons peeled and grated fresh ginger
½ teaspoon red pepper flakes
1 tablespoon grapeseed oil
1 large onion, chopped
2 large carrots, sliced
1 large red bell pepper, sliced
1 large green bell pepper, sliced
4 cloves garlic, minced
½ pound mushrooms, sliced
1 small zucchini, sliced

- To prepare marinade: Combine fish sauce, ketchup, agave nectar, and lime juice in a large container. Add the sliced sirloin steak and let marinate for 30 minutes.
- Remove the meat from the marinade and set aside. Combine the remaining marinade with the arrowroot, vegetable broth, ginger, and crushed red pepper. Set aside.
- Heat a large skillet over medium-high heat and heat the oil. Sauté the onion, carrots, bell peppers, and garlic for 4 to 6 minutes, or until tender. Add the mushrooms and zucchini, and sauté for 2 minutes longer. Remove from the skillet. Add the meat to the skillet and cook until done, 3 to 4 minutes.
- Whisk the marinade mixture and add to the skillet. Once the mixture has thickened add the vegetables and heat through. Serve this dish over hot brown rice.

nutritional analysis per serving
190.27 calories; 7.53 g fat (35% calories from fat); 15.42 g protein; 17.0 g carbohydrate; 37.62 mg cholesterol; 1049.83 mg sodium

Bell Peppers Stuffed with Quinoa

PREP TIME: 30 minutes to prepare and 10 to 15 minutes to bake
SERVE: Serves 4

Quinoa is such a wonderful source of protein, and it tastes so good too. It is light, fluffy, and has a slightly nutty flavor. It's easy to digest, contains all of the amino acids, and is a rich source of iron. You'll love it in this recipe.

4 large red bell peppers (or yellow, orange, or green)

1½ cups vegetable or chicken broth

½ teaspoon salt

¾ cup quinoa, rinsed and drained

2 teaspoons olive oil

1 cup red onion, chopped finely

½ teaspoon ground cumin

¼ cup chopped cilantro

1 tablespoon lime juice

¼ cup currants

½ cup pine nuts

Salt

½ teaspoon freshly ground pepper

- Preheat the oven to 450°F. Spray a cookie sheet with olive oil and cut the bell peppers in half and seed. Place them cut side down on the sheet and bake for 10 to 12 minutes, or until tender. Reduce oven temperature to 350°F

- In a saucepan, combine the vegetable broth, salt, and quinoa; bring to a boil. Turn the heat to low and simmer until done, about 10 minutes. Quinoa should be light and fluffy. If it is not, cook for 1 to 2 minutes longer.

- In a large skillet, heat the olive oil and add the onions. Cook until soft, 4 to 5 minutes. Add the cumin and continue cooking for 1 minute. Add the cilantro, lime juice, quinoa mixture, currants, and pine nuts. Toss to mix well. Season with salt and pepper. Stuff into the pepper halves and place on a cookie sheet. Bake at 350°F for 10 minutes, or until heated through.

nutritional analysis per serving
389.00 calories; 16.40 g fat (34% calories from fat); 15.40 g protein; 54.0 g carbohydrate; 0 mg cholesterol; 960.1 mg sodium

Cabbage Rolls

NO DAIRY OR NUTS

PREP TIME: 20 minutes to prepare and 50 minutes to cook.
SERVE: Serves 4

This is another of my grandmother's recipes. It's no wonder she lived to ninety-eight years of age she ate from the garden, and always incorporated vegetables into our meals. This dish was one of her favorites.

1 large head cabbage
2 tablespoons canola oil
1 medium-size onion, chopped
2 cloves garlic, minced
1 pound ground turkey (or buffalo)
1 cup cooked brown rice
1 egg, beaten
¼ cup dried dill
½ teaspoon salt
¼ teaspoon pepper
12 ounces tomatoes, crushed
3 tablespoons balsamic vinegar
1 tablespoon agave nectar or fruit sweetener

- Preheat the oven to 350°F.
- Wash the cabbage and remove the core. Steam over high heat until the cabbage leaves are tender, about 12 minutes. Set aside.
- In a small saucepan, heat the oil over medium heat and add the chopped onion and garlic. Sauté until soft, 4 to 5 minutes.
- In a medium-size bowl, combine the meat, rice, beaten egg, dill, salt, and pepper.
- Place ⅓ cup of the meat mixture on each cabbage leaf and roll up like a jelly roll. Place in a 9-inch square baking dish. Continue until the mixture is used up.
- Heat the tomatoes, vinegar, and agave nectar together in a small saucepan and pour over the cabbage rolls. Cover and bake for 40 to 50 minutes.

nutritional analysis per serving
414.22 calories; 11.83 g fat (26% calories from fat); 15.06 g protein; 68.73 g carbohydrate; 74.94 mg cholesterol; 226.61 mg sodium

Chicken Cacciatore

PREP/COOK TIME: 40 minutes
SERVE: Serves 4

Sunday afternoons used to be the time I prepared meals for the week. The kids are grown and gone now, and I don't need to prepare for the week ahead, as I now work from home. I used to make this recipe on those long forgotten Sunday afternoons, and I can still remember the kids running around the house as I was chopping the veggies and stirring the pot.

1 tablespoon olive oil

2 chicken breasts, washed and cut into 1-inch pieces

1 large onion, chopped finely

½ red bell pepper, chopped

3 cloves garlic, chopped

1 small zucchini, cut into cubes

½ small leek, chopped

1 cup mushrooms, sliced

1 (14½-ounce) can stewed tomatoes with basil and oregano

1 cup tomato sauce

1 teaspoon fresh rosemary, crumbled

½ teaspoon salt

¼ teaspoon freshly ground pepper

- In a large cooking pot or Dutch oven, heat olive oil. Add chicken breasts and sauté for 6 to 7 minutes, or until browned. Remove from pot and set aside.
- Chop the onion, red bell pepper, garlic, zucchini, and leek. Slice the mushrooms. Add to the Dutch oven and sauté over medium heat for 5 to 10 minutes, or until soft. Add the tomatoes with juice, tomato sauce, chicken, and fresh rosemary. Let this simmer, covered, for 10 minutes. Add the salt and pepper and serve.

> I serve this over wild rice or polenta. Either way it is delicious!

nutritional analysis per serving
246.71 calories; 5.42 g fat (19% calories from fat); 30.70 g protein; 19.30 g carbohydrate; 68.44 mg cholesterol; 638.53 mg sodium

Falafels

PREP/COOK TIME: 20 minutes
SERVE: Serves 4

I love the flavor of falafels. They are spicy, but not too spicy, and provide a great source of protein. You can serve them on a bed of lettuce, inside a lettuce wrap, or as an appetizer.

¼ cup canola oil

1 large onion, chopped

¼ cup chopped parsley

2 cloves garlic, minced

2 (15-ounce) cans garbanzo beans, drained (reserve juice)

¼ cup quinoa flour

1 tablespoon wheat-free tamari sauce

4 tablespoons chopped fresh coriander

½ teaspoon ground turmeric

½ teaspoon ground cumin

½ teaspoon garlic powder

1 recipe Falafel Saouce (page 188)

- Preheat the oven to 350°F if you prefer to bake rather than fry the falafel.
- In large skillet, heat 1 tablespoon of the oil and sauté the onion until soft. Add the parsley and garlic, and continue cooking for 1 minute.
- In a blender or food processor, combine the rest of the ingredients except the oil and blend.
- Add the onion mixture and form into patties. If the mixture is too dry, add a little of the reserved garbanzo bean juice.
- Heat 1 tablespoon of the oil in the skillet over medium heat. Add one patty at a time and sauté until done, about 3 minutes on each side. Drain on paper towels. Continue this process until all of the patties are cooked. Or, if you would rather bake the patties, place them on a cookie sheet that has been lightly oiled and bake for about 30 minutes, turning each patty over after baking 15 minutes.
- Serve with Falafel Sauce.

nutritional analysis per serving
441.86 calories; 16.39 g fat (33% calories from fat); 13.15 g protein; 61.39 g carbohydrate; 0 mg cholesterol; 932.96 mg sodium

Fried Oysters

PREP/COOK TIME: 30 minutes
SERVE: Serves 4

Growing up on the beach in the Pacific Northwest, we often ate oysters. I know fried foods are bad for us, but once in a great while they sure taste good. If you don't have rice crackers, substitute crushed cornflakes. Nobody will know the difference.

1 pint extra-small oysters

1 cup rice flour or crushed rice crackers

2 tablespoons chopped parsley

½ teaspoon salt

¼ teaspoon ground fresh pepper

2 eggs, beaten

3 tablespoons grapeseed or canola oil

- Rinse and drain the oysters. If using rice flour, mix it along with the parsley, salt, and pepper in a shallow pan. If using rice crackers, crush them with a rolling pin and combine with the parsley, salt, and pepper.
- Dip the oysters into the beaten eggs, then into the flour mixture. Heat a skillet over medium-high heat. Heat the oil a tablespoon at a time, and fry the oysters a few at a time. Fry until the oysters are browned and cooked through. Drain on paper towels. Continue this process, adding more oil and oysters until all of the oysters have been cooked. Serve hot.

nutritional analysis per serving
245.83 calories; 13.34 g fat (48% of calories from fat); 6.16 g protein; 24.76 g carbohydrate; 112.00 mg cholesterol; 340.36 mg sodium

Ginger Turkey Meatballs

PREP/COOK TIME: 30 to 35 minutes
SERVE: Serves 4

I made these meatballs recently and didn't have any rice crackers on hand. I substituted cornflakes and I couldn't even tell the difference. These meatballs store well in the fridge or freezer.

1½ pounds ground turkey

1 large egg, beaten

1 small carrot, grated

¼ cup small onions, chopped finely

⅓ cup rice crackers

2 cloves garlic, chopped

1 tablespoon peeled and grated fresh ginger

¼ teaspoon salt

¼ teaspoon pepper

1 tablespoon olive oil

Water as needed

- Place the ground turkey in a large bowl, add the egg, and mix together. Add the grated carrot and onion to the meat mixture. Using a rolling pin, crush the crackers in a resealable plastic bag and add to the meat mixture. Add the ginger, salt, and pepper. Mix well.

- Form into small balls. In a large skillet, heat the oil and cook the meatballs, turning often, until all sides are browned. Turn down the heat, add a little water to the skillet so the meatballs do not stick, and cover with a lid. Simmer for 10 to 15 minutes or until the meatballs are cooked through.

nutritional analysis per serving
338.72 calories; 18.94 g fat (50% of calories from fat); 32.41 g protein; 7.95 g carbohydrate; 187.25 mg cholesterol; 383.89 mg sodium

Greek-Style Lettuce Wraps

NO EGGS OR NUTS

PREP TIME: 10 minutes
SERVE: Serves 4

This is a salad in a wrap. You can use rice noodle wraps, too, but why add more carbohydrates? Lettuce wraps are a great way to replace glutenous foods such as tortillas or pita bread.

½ cup feta cheese

1 large ripe avocado, chopped

½ cup finely chopped green onions

1 small cucumber, sliced in half and then cubed

3 tablespoons sliced black olives

1 small red bell pepper, sliced thinly

2 tablespoons yogurt or mayonnaise

2 large tomatoes, sliced

2 teaspoons lime juice

½ teaspoon freshly ground pepper

4 large romaine lettuce leaves, washed and drained

- In a large salad bowl, combine all the ingredients except the lettuce.
- Place a lettuce leaf on each serving plate and scoop the salad mixture into the lettuce wrap. Roll, cabbage-roll style, turning in the ends so the salad does not fall out. Serve.

nutritional analysis per serving
189.80 calories; 14.06 g fat (63% calories from fat); 5.69 g protein; 13.74 g carbohydrate; 17.15 mg cholesterol; 285.07 mg sodium

Grilled Eggplant Parmesan

NO EGGS OR NUTS (AND CAN BE MADE NONDAIRY)

PREP TIME: 45 minutes to prepare and about 30 minutes to bake

SERVE: Serves 6

I love eggplant Parmesan, but in the old days, I fried the eggplant after dipping it in egg and bread crumbs. Today, I grill my eggplant and omit the eggs and flour. It's much healthier and reduces the calorie count considerably. Now I can eat it without the guilt.

2 pounds eggplant

Salt, plus more to taste

3 tablespoons olive oil

3 cups tomato sauce

Pepper to taste

¾ pound mozzarella cheese, grated (or nondairy mozzarella cheese)

1 cup Parmesan cheese (or nondairy Parmesan cheese)

4 teaspoon oregano, fresh if possible

Pepper, to taste

1 recipe Pesto (page 93) or, if you prefer nondairy, Tofu Pesto (page 193) (optional)

- Peel eggplant and slice into 3/8-inch pieces. Sprinkle salt on each side and drain on paper towels for about 20 minutes. Turn over and drain on the other side for 20 minutes. Rinse and pat dry.
- Preheat the oven to 350°F.
- Drizzle the oil on eggplant and then grill for 3 to 4 minutes on each side, or until lightly browned.
- Combine the oregano, tomato sauce, salt, and pepper, and pour a small amount on the bottom of a 9 × 13-inch pan. Layer the eggplant, sauce and slices of mozzarella cheese, and sprinkle with the Parmesan. Continue layering until you have used all the eggplant, sauce, and cheese, ending with cheese.
- Bake for about 30 minutes, or until bubbly. Remove from the oven and let it sit for 5 minutes. Top with a pesto sauce, optional and serve with a green salad, if desired.

nutritional analysis per serving
264.65 calories; 15.86 g fat (53% calories from fat); 17.53 g protein; 15.18 g carbohydrate; 38.22 mg cholesterol; 994.02 mg sodium

Grilled Halibut with Pesto Sauce

NO EGGS OR NUTS

PREP TIME: 10 minutes to prepare and 10 minutes to cook
SERVE: Serves 4

Pesto is so easy to make and goes with so many dishes. Don't limit this pesto to just halibut; it's great over rice noodles, served with the eggplant Parmesan, or over pizza dough, just to name a few.

4 (4-ounce) halibut steaks
Dash of olive oil for brushing on fish

Pesto Sauce:

2 tablespoons olive oil
¼ cup packed fresh basil, chopped
3 tablespoons grated Parmesan cheese
2 cloves garlic, chopped
Dash of salt
¼ teaspoon freshly ground pepper

- Heat the grill and lightly brush the halibut steaks with olive oil. Grill the halibut until done, about 5 minutes on each side.
- Prepare the Pesto: In a blender combine the oil, fresh basil, Parmesan cheese, garlic, salt, and pepper. Puree until smooth.
- Serve the pesto on the side with the grilled fish.

nutritional analysis per serving
253.75 calories; 10.06 g fat (35% calories from fat); 36.28 g protein; 3.48 g carbohydrate; 103.66 mg cholesterol; 173.25 mg sodium

Grilled Lamb Chops
with Lemon-Basil Spread

NO DAIRY, EGGS, OR NUTS

PREP TIME: 70 minutes to prepare (including marinating time) and 10 minutes to cook
SERVE: Serves 4

You have to prepare this recipe in advance to allow enough time for it to marinate in the refrigerator, but it's worth it. Serve this along with a salad and fresh green bean, and you'll have a scrumptious meal waiting for you.

¼ cup lemon juice

½ teaspoon thyme leaves

1 tablespoon olive oil

2 cloves garlic, minced

4 lamb chops (1¼–1½-inch thick)

1 cup fresh basil, washed and chopped

¼ cup shortening, melted

1 tablespoon lemon zest

Salt

Pepper

- Place the lemon juice, thyme, olive oil, and garlic in a large resealable bag. Shake to mix well. Add the lamb chops and shake to cover with the marinade. Place in the refrigerator for 1 hour.
- To make the basil spread, combine all the ingredients (basil, shortening, and grated lemon zest) in a blender and process until well blended and smooth, about 2 minutes. Put in a small bowl, cover, and refrigerate for up to an hour.
- Preheat the grill or broiler and remove the meat from the marinade. Grill the chops for about 5 minutes on each side (depending on thickness). Season with salt and pepper and serve with the lemon-basil spread.

nutritional analysis per serving
594.13 calories; 51.19 g fat (78% calories from fat); 29.17 g protein; 2.62 g carbohydrate; 122.47 mg cholesterol; 219.82 mg sodium

Hot and Spicy Chicken with Peanuts

NO DAIRY OR EGGS

PREP TIME: About 60 minutes to marinate and 30 minutes to cook
SERVE: Serves 6

This recipe does contain peanuts, so if you have a peanut allergy, substitute cashews and replace the peanut oil with grapeseed oil or olive oil. This dish takes some time to prepare, but it's well worth the effort.

1½ pound chicken breasts, skinless and boneless, cut into 1-inch cubes

2 tablespoons peanut oil

1 cup water chestnuts

½ cup unsalted peanuts

Marinade:

1 teaspoon sesame oil

1 teaspoon arrowroot

2 tablespoons wheat-free tamari sauce

2 tablespoons sherry or red wine

Vegetables:

4–5 cloves garlic, minced

1 tablespoon peeled and minced or grated fresh ginger

3 green onions, chopped

1 red bell pepper, chopped

Chicken sauce:

½ cup chicken broth

1 tablespoon brown rice syrup

2 tablespoons wheat-free tamari sauce

2 tablespoons Worcestershire sauce

1–1½ teaspoons arrowroot

■ Begin by making the marinade. Combine the ingredients and place in a resealable plastic bag or a large bowl with lid. Add the chicken and marinate in the refrigerator for an hour.

■ In the meantime, mix together the garlic, ginger, green onions, and red bell pepper. Set aside. Mix all ingredients for the chicken sauce in a separate bowl and set that aside, too.

■ Take the chicken out of the marinade, reserving the marinade. Place the chicken in a medium-size skillet that has been heated over medium-high heat. Sauté, turning often, for about 5 minutes, or until cooked through. Set aside.

■ In a large skillet, heat the peanut oil, add the vegetables, and sauté for 2 to 3 minutes. Add the chicken sauce and cook for 1 to 2 minutes or until the mixture is thick. Keep stirring to avoid burning. Add the cooked chicken and toss to cover well. Next, add the water chestnuts and the peanuts. Heat through and serve.

■ Serve this over brown rice or rice noodles. It is very good either way.

nutritional analysis per serving
266.52 calories; 15.46 g fat (49% calories from fat); 12.20 g protein; 23.21 g carbohydrate; 10.30 mg cholesterol; 456.67 mg sodium

Layered Polenta

NO EGGS OR NUTS

PREP TIME: 10 to 15 minutes to prepare and 15 to 20 minutes to bake
SERVE: Serves 6

I love polenta *for many reasons, but mainly because you can do so much with it. You can add ingredients into the polenta itself, or you can top it with meats, veggies, or sauces. It is very versatile and hearty. This is made like a meat loaf, in a loaf pan that you invert after baking. It's fun to make and tastes wonderful.*

½ small onion, chopped

1 clove garlic, chopped

½ pound spinach, chopped finely

7 ounces pesto sauce (see page 93)

1 cup oil-packed sun-dried tomatoes, drained and chopped

2 large tomatoes, chopped

6 cups water

½ teaspoon salt

2 cups cornmeal

¼ pound Swiss cheese, grated

2 tablespoons grated Parmesan cheese

½ teaspoon ground black pepper

- Preheat the oven to 350°F. Sauté the onions in a small skillet until soft. Add the garlic and sauté 1 minute longer.
- In a medium-size bowl combine the spinach, and the sautéed onion mixture with the pesto sauce. In small bowl, combine the dried and fresh tomatoes.
- In a saucepan, bring the water and salt to a boil. Gradually add the cornmeal, stirring constantly. Reduce the heat and cook until thick, about 10 minutes. Remove from heat and add the Swiss cheese. Stir until all the cheese has melted. Set aside.
- Line a 9 × 5-inch loaf pan with foil. Spread the bottom of the pan with some of the cornmeal mixture. Top with the tomato mixture, then more polenta, and finally, the spinach and pesto mixture. Sprinkle with the Parmesan cheese, pinch the foil edges together, and bake for 15 to 20 minutes. Remove from the oven and carefully lift the entire loaf from the pan. Unfold the foil and carefully invert on a serving platter. Let sit 5 minutes and serve.

nutritional analysis per serving
456.72 calories; 26.42 g fat (50% calories from fat); 16.95 g protein; 41.86 g carbohydrate; 28.95 mg cholesterol; 415.26 mg sodium

Marinated Flank Steak

PREP/COOK TIME: 40 minutes
SERVE: Serves 4

Flank steak is a tough meat, so you have to either beat it or marinate it to tenderize it. I prefer to marinate it and then grill it. You can broil it if the weather is not conducive to grilling. This recipe pairs well with roasted vegetables and a salad. Cut it into thin strips before serving.

⅓ cup sherry or red wine

¼ cup ketchup

2 tablespoons tamari sauce

1 tablespoon olive oil

1 tablespoon Worcestershire sauce

1 tablespoon brown rice syrup

1 teaspoon Dijon mustard

2 cloves garlic

½ teaspoon dried thyme

¼ teaspoon pepper

½ teaspoon driedparsley

1½ pounds flank steak

- Combine all of the ingredients except the flank steak in a large resealable plastic bag. Shake well to mix all the ingredients together. (You can use a large baking dish if you prefer, rather than the bag. Point is, get the meat in the sauce for as long as you can.) Add the flank steak and marinate in the sauce for at least 2 hours in the refrigerator.

- Remove from the bag, and heat the grill or broiler. Reserve the marinade for later. Broil or grill the flank steak on each side for 6 minutes, or until it reaches your preferred doneness.

- Pour the marinade ingredients into a saucepan and heat to boiling. Reduce the heat and continue to cook until the mixture has reduced by half. Serve over the flank steak.

nutritional analysis per serving
154.25 calories; 4.28 g fat (4.28% calories from fat); 5.47 g protein; 19.69 g carbohydrate; 7.00 mg cholesterol; 597.89 mg sodium

Marinated Halibut

PREP TIME: 1 hour
SERVE: Serves 4

Asian flavors spring to life in this recipe. Add fresh grated ginger if you wish to add more spice. Serve with Egg Drop Soup (page 60) and Cauliflower Curry (page 168) for a spicy, well-rounded meal.

4 (6-ounce) halibut fillets
1 tablespoon grapeseed oil

Marinade:

1 tablespoon brown rice syrup
1 tablespoon Asian fish sauce
1 tablespoon tamari sauce
2 tablespoons lemon or orange juice
2 cloves garlic, minced
2 tablespoons minced cilantro
1 teaspoon sesame oil

- Combine all of the marinade ingredients in a bowl. Add the fish and cover. (You can also place all of the ingredients in a resealable plastic bag and shake. Marinate the fish in the refrigerator for 30 minutes.

- Heat a large skillet over medium high-heat and add the oil. When it is hot, add the fish, flesh side down (set the marinade aside). Cook for about 4 minutes, or until well browned. Turn the fish over and cook for another 4 to 5 minutes. Add the marinade and continue cooking, covered, for about 5 minutes or until the fish is flaky. Do not overcook.

- Serve over wild rice.

nutritional analysis per serving
302.15 calories; 11.63 g fat (35% calories from fat); 38.94 g protein; 9.51 g carbohydrate; 118.80 mg cholesterol; 708.93 mg sodium

Meatballs

PREP/COOK TIME: 50 minutes to prepare
SERVE: Serves 6

I prefer to eat bison/buffalo over beef due to the fact that it contains less fat. It is a lean meat with very good taste. It is not gamey like some meats. You can typically find it at a high-end gourmet grocery store, or a local meat market. You can substitute beef in this recipe if you don't want to use either the turkey or bison.

1 pound buffalo meat or ground turkey

½ onion, chopped

½ cup cornflakes or rice crackers, crushed

2 eggs, beaten

Salt and pepper, to taste

2 tablespoons olive oil

¼ cup water

- In a large bowl, mix together all the ingredients except the oil and water; form into balls.
- Heat the olive oil in a large nonstick skillet and brown the balls on all sides. Turn the heat to medium-low, add the water, cover, and simmer until the meatballs are done.

nutritional analysis per serving
157.19 calories; 7.48 g fat (42% calories from fat); 18.14 g protein; 3.44 g carbohydrate; 116.56 mg cholesterol; 115.91 mg sodium

Moussaka

PREP TIME: 20 minutes to prepare and 45 minutes to bake
SERVE: Serves 8

I love Greek food, and this is a wonderful dish.

1 medium-size eggplant, washed and peeled, cut into ½-inch slices

3 tablespoons olive oil

2 medium-size red onions, chopped

6 mushrooms, sliced

2 cloves garlic, chopped

1 medium-size zucchini, sliced thinly

1 pound ground lamb

1 cup tomato sauce

¼ cup red wine

1 teaspoon ground cinnamon

1 cup ricotta cheese

3 egg yolks, lightly beaten

2 tablespoons butter

1½ tablespoons arrowroot

1½ cups nonfat milk

⅓ cup grated Parmesan cheese

- Preheat the oven to 350°F.
- Heat 2 tablespoons of the olive oil over medium heat in a skillet. Brown the eggplant and drain. Add, if necessary, 1 more tablespoon of olive oil and sauté the onions, garlic, and mushrooms. Add the zucchini and sauté for about 2 minutes. Add the ground lamb. Cook through (5–6 minutes). Stir in tomato sauce, wine, cinnamon, ricotta cheese, half the egg yolks, and salt and pepper.
- In a small saucepan, heat the butter, stir in the arrowroot, and cook for 1 minute. Stir in the milk and cook until the sauce is thick and smooth. Stir in the remaining egg yolks. Spread half the eggplant in a baking dish. Top with the meat. Place the rest of the eggplant on top. Pour the cream sauce over the top. Sprinkle with the Parmesan cheese. Bake for 45 minutes.

nutritional analysis per serving
343.92 calories; 21.95 g fat (52% calories from fat); 20.26 g protein; 18.09 g carbohydrate; 138.41 mg cholesterol; 347.10 mg sodium

Nut Loaf

PREP TIME: 10 minutes to prepare and up to 40 minutes to bake

SERVE: Serves 6

If you want, you can use hazelnuts or almonds in place of the walnuts for this delicious loaf. I like to use lots of freshly ground pepper, but start with the amount listed, and add more if you wish.

2 tablespoons olive oil

1 large onion, chopped

1 tablespoon arrowroot or brown rice flour

1 teaspoon dried thyme

¾ cup water

1 cup walnuts, chopped finely

1 cup cashews, chopped finely

1 cup crushed rice crackers

1 tablespoon orange or lemon juice

½ teaspoon salt

¼ teaspoon freshly ground pepper

2 cloves garlic, minced

- Preheat the oven to 400°F.
- Heat a large skillet to medium-high and add the oil and onions. Sauté until soft, 4 to 5 minutes. Add the garlic and cook for 1 minute. Add the arrowroot, thyme, and water. Cook for 2 minutes, or until thickened. Add the nuts, and crushed crackers (I use rice crackers, but you can use rice cereal, millet cereal, or cornflakes.). Remove from the heat and add the orange juice, salt, and pepper. Blend until well mixed and all the ingredients are moistened.
- Press into a greased loaf pan and bake for 30 to 40 minutes, depending on the size of the pan (a standard 8 × 3-inch pan works best).
- Remove from pan and slice before serving.

nutritional analysis per serving
SBH314.72 calories; 25.41 g fat (68% calories from fat); 7.60 g protein; 18.16 g carbohydrate; 0 mg cholesterol; 106.51 mg sodium

One-Pot Stew

NO DAIRY, EGGS, OR NUTS

PREP/COOK TIME: 5 hours
SERVE: Serves 5 to 6

This is one of my father's favorite recipes because it is so easy to make. You simply put everything together in the stew pot and let it cook. Simple, yet hearty. I hope you will enjoy. Feel free to add ½ cup quinoa or rice if you wish. This dish is also delicious served over polenta.

4 large carrots, peeled and cut into 2-inch chunks

1 large onion, quartered

3 large red potatoes, peeled and quartered

3 large cloves garlic, peeled and cut in half

½ pound mushrooms (any variety), washed

1½ pounds top sirloin round steak, cubed

½ cup red or white wine

1 (15-ounce) can organic tomato sauce

1 cup hot water

1½ tablespoons arrowroot

½ teaspoon salt

½ teaspoon freshly ground pepper

1 teaspoon ground cumin

Dash of red pepper flakes

- Preheat the oven to 250°F.
- Place all of the ingredients (except the arrowroot and hot water) in the pot. Add the arrowroot to the hot water and stir until the powder dissolves. Add to the pot and cover. Place in the oven and cook very slowly for 4 to 5 hours. Do not disturb during the cooking process.

> Can also be made in a Crock-Pot.

nutritional analysis per serving
400.12 calories; 7.55 g fat (17% calories from fat); 35.25 g protein; 45.88 g carbohydrate; 83.01 mg cholesterol; 882.11 mg sodium

Pan-Seared Sea Bass with Peach Salsa

NO DAIRY, EGGS, OR NUTS

PREP/COOK TIME: 1 hour and 15 minutes
SERVE: Serves 4

Sea bass is a white fish, so you can substitute any other white fish in this recipe. I love fresh peaches in summer, so this is a perfect summer evening entrée.

4 (6-ounce) sea bass fillets
Olive oil (enough to coat fillets)

Salsa:

1 large peach, chopped

1 large avocado, chopped

½ small red onion, chopped finely

½ cup red bell pepper, diced

2 teaspoons peeled and grated fresh ginger

2 tablespoons chopped cilantro

2 tablespoons olive oil

1 tablespoon brown rice syrup

3 tablespoons lime juice

½ teaspoon ground cumin

¼ teaspoon freshly ground pepper

- In a medium-size bowl, combine the peach, avocado, onion, pepper, ginger, and cilantro. In a small bowl, whisk together the olive oil, brown rice syrup, lime juice, cumin, and pepper. Pour over the peach mixture and toss to coat. Refrigerate for 1 hour before serving.
- Heat the grill. To prepare the sea bass, rub the fillets with the olive oil and place on grill. Cook for 5 to 6 minutes on each side. Sprinkle with salt and pepper. Serve with the salsa.

nutritional analysis per serving
283.10 calories; 12.87 g fat (39% calories from fat); 22.28 g protein; 20.48 g carbohydrate; 46.47 mg cholesterol; 88.90 mg sodium

Polenta

NO EGGS OR NUTS

PREP TIME: 15 minutes to prepare and 30 minutes to bake
SERVE: Serves 10

This simple version of polenta can be
pared with the Vegetable Ragout (page
106), Ratatouille (page 112), or a number of other recipes. It's a great base
on which to build. Use your imagination, and have fun with it!

4 cups milk (or substitute
   unsweetened soy milk)

1 cup water

1¼ cups coarse polenta (cornmeal)

¼ teaspoon salt

½ cup grated Parmesan cheese
   (omit if you want this dairy-
   free)

- Combine the milk and water in a saucepan
  and bring to a boil. Slowly add the polenta
  and reduce heat. Continue cooking for about
  10 minutes, or until thick. Add the salt and
  Parmesan; remove from heat.
- Preheat oven to 350°F and coat a 9-inch pie
  pan or square pan with cooking oil. Pour the
  polenta into the pan and bake for 30 minutes.
  Remove from the oven and let cool.

nutritional analysis per serving
146.11 calories; 4.47 g fat (27% calories from fat);
7.46 g protein; 19.45 g carbohydrate; 5.50 mg cholesterol; 187.23 mg sodium

Vegetable Ragout

PREP/COOK TIME: 15 minutes
SERVE: Serves 6

This ragout is served best over the Polenta found on page 97, but you can serve it over rice or pasta as well. I love Mediterranean food, so I make this dish often. It's full of protein but low on calories and fat.

3 tablespoons olive oil

1 large onion, chopped

½ pound eggplant, peeled and cubed

½ pound zucchini, chopped

2 pounds butternut squash, washed, peeled, and cubed

1 (28-ounce) can diced tomatoes

¼ cup minced garlic

1 pound spinach, chopped

½ cup fresh basil

Salt and pepper, to taste

2 (i5-ounce) cans white beans (cannellini)

■ Heat the oil in a large Dutch oven or skillet, and sauté the onion for 4 to 5 minutes over medium heat until the onion is soft. Add the eggplant, zucchini, and squash. Sauté for another 4 to 5 minutes. Add the tomatoes, garlic, and spinach; reduce heat to medium-low. Add the beans. Cover and cook until the vegetables are tender but not overcooked. Add the basil, salt, and pepper, and serve over hot polenta.

nutritional analysis per serving
146.11 calories; 4.47 g fat (27% calories from fat); 7.46 g protein; 19.45 g carbohydrate; 5.50 mg cholesterol; 187.23 mg sodium

Pork Chops with a Kick

NO DAIRY, EGGS, OR NUTS

PREP/COOK TIME: 15 to 20 minutes
SERVE: Serves 4

If you want to give these chops more of a kick, add more chile powder. That will spice them up and give you some heat! Shallots add a nice flavor but if you can't find them, use leeks, or even onions will suffice. You can also broil these chops instead of grilling, if you prefer.

1 teaspoon olive oil

1 teaspoon chile powder

1 tablespoon peeled and grated fresh ginger

2 teaspoons ground coriander

4 cloves garlic, minced

½ teaspoon salt

¼ teaspoon freshly ground black pepper

2 tablespoons agave nectar or brown rice syrup

4 (4-ounce) boneless pork chops (½-inch thick)

2 tablespoons minced shallots

- In a large bowl, combine all the ingredients except the chops, oil, and shallots.
- Score the chops and rub the mixture into the meat.
- Preheat the grill and cook the chops for 4 to 5 minutes on each side, or until done. If you do not have a grill, cook on the stovetop with a small amount of olive oil in a large skillet.
- In a small saucepan, sauté the shallots in the olive oil until crisp.
- Serve over polenta or rice, topped with the sautéed shallots.

nutritional analysis per serving

171.01 calories; 2.91 g fat (15% calories from fat); 25.97 g protein; 10.53 g carbohydrate; 62.37 mg cholesterol; 507.58 mg sodium

Portobello Mushroom Pizza

NO EGGS OR NUTS

PREP/COOK TIME: 20 minutes
SERVE: Serves 4

Portobello mushrooms can be used for so many recipes. They can serve as the foundation of a dish, as they are used here, or in a sauce, or as a garnish. You'll love how easy these are to make and how versatile this recipe is. Instead of making an Italian-style pizza, how about a Southwest version topped with green onions, red bell peppers, black olives, sautéed chicken, and Monterey Jack cheese?

1½ teaspoons olive oil

1 small onion, chopped

½ cup spinach, washed and chopped finely

1 cup chopped tomatoes

4 cloves garlic, chopped

2 tablespoons black olives, drained and sliced

½ teaspoon dried oregano

2 tablespoons dried basil

½ teaspoon salt

¼ teaspoon pepper

4 medium-size portobello mushrooms

Light oil as needed

½ cup mozzarella cheese

- Heat the oil in a large skillet and add the onion. Sauté for 4 minutes or until soft. Add the spinach, tomatoes, garlic, and olives. Continue to sauté for about 3 minutes longer.
- Add the oregano, basil, salt, and pepper, and mix well. Remove from the heat.
- Preheat the broiler and prepare the mushrooms by removing the stems and wiping off any dirt. Brush or spray the mushrooms with a light oil and place on a cookie sheet. Broil on each side for 4 minutes, or until soft. Remove from the heat and fill with the vegetable mixture. Sprinkle the mozzarella cheese on top and return to the broiler for another 4 to 5 minutes. Serve hot. This dish and a big green salad make a hearty meal.

nutritional analysis per serving
113.93 calories; 5.19 g fat (40% calories from fat); 7.69 g protein; 11.80 g carbohydrate; 10.56 mg cholesterol; 442.20 mg sodium

Potato Curry

PREP/COOK TIME: 20 to 30 minutes
SERVE: Serves 4

If you love the flavor of Indian food, and the smell of curry in your kitchen, you'll love this dish. It warms you through and through. This can be served by itself, as a side dish, or over red rice or lentils for a heartier meal.

4 large Finnish yellow potatoes, cut into 1-inch pieces

1 large onion, chopped

5 cloves garlic, chopped

1 tablespoon peeled and chopped fresh ginger

1 cup water

1 teaspoon ground turmeric

½ teaspoon ground coriander

½ teaspoon ground cumin

¼ cup grapeseed or canola oil

1 tablespoon sesame oil

½ cup chopped cilantro

- In a blender or food processor, combine the chopped onion with the garlic, ginger, and up to ½ cup water, if needed. Blend until smooth. Add the turmeric, coriander, and cumin. Heat the grapeseed oil in a large skillet over medium heat and add the onion mixture. This mixture may stick in the pan, so continue to add small amounts of water to avoid sticking or burning.

- Add the potatoes, the rest of the water, and the sesame oil to the skillet. Stir to coat the potatoes completely, and lower the heat. Over medium-low heat, simmer 10–12 minutes or until the potatoes are tender, adding more water if needed.

- Remove from the heat and stir in the chopped cilantro. Serve immediately.

nutritional analysis per serving

118.31 calories; 3.72 g fat (28% calories from fat); 2.31 g protein; 19.63 g carbohydrate; 0 mg cholesterol; 50.15 mg sodium

Prosciutto and Veggies

NO DAIRY, EGGS, OR NUTS

PREP/COOK TIME: 20 to 25 minutes
SERVE: Serves 6

Prosciutto is an Italian aged, dry cured spiced ham that is cut paper-thin. It has a wonderful flavor and blends well with this recipe.

1 cup broccoli, chopped

1 cup Brussels sprouts, cut in half and trimmed

1 cup asparagus, cut into 1-inch pieces

2 tablespoons olive oil

1 ounce prosciutto, chopped

½ teaspoon salt

¼ teaspoon freshly ground pepper

1 tablespoon balsamic vinegar

- In a small saucepan, steam or boil the broccoli, Brussels sprouts, and asparagus.
- In a large skillet, heat 1 tablespoon of the oil and sauté the prosciutto until crisp, 5 to 7 minutes, stirring occasionally. Remove from the skillet and add the broccoli, Brussels sprouts, and asparagus. You may need to add another tablespoon of olive oil. Sauté the veggies over medium-high heat until tender and slightly browned. Add the prosciutto, salt, pepper, and balsamic vinegar. Serve immediately.

nutritional analysis per serving
79.08 calories; 5.50 g fat (62% calories from fat); 4.66 g protein; 4.02 g carbohydrate; 6.61 mg cholesterol; 634.29 mg sodium

Quinoa and Tofu

PREP TIME: 40 minutes
SERVE: Serves 4

Tofu and quinoa, *two great sources of protein, team up with a few vegetables to provide a hearty side dish. Feel free to add other vegetables to this, or toss in a few red pepper flakes to give it some heat!*

1 cup vegetable stock
1 cup quinoa
8 ounces extra-firm tofu
2 teaspoons olive oil
1 small red onion, chopped finely
1 medium-size red bell pepper, sliced
1 tablespoon chopped garlic

■ Heat the vegetable stock in a medium-size saucepan until boiling. Add the quinoa and reduce the heat. Simmer for 15 to 20 minutes, or until the quinoa is light and fluffy.

■ While the quinoa is cooking, drain the tofu on paper towels (15 to 20 minutes). Cut into cubes.

■ In a medium-size skillet, heat oil and sauté the onion and pepper for 5 to 6 minutes. Add the cubed tofu and garlic, and continue to sauté for another 3 to 4 minutes. Add the cooked quinoa, pepper, and parsley. Toss until well blended.

nutritional analysis per serving
270.59 calories; 8.57 g fat (26% calories from fat);
12.80 g protein; 38.74 g carbohydrate; 0 mg cholesterol;
50.68 mg sodium

Ratatouille

PREP/COOK TIME: 1½ hours
SERVE: Serves 8

This is such a hearty stew. It lacks sufficient protein for a complete meal, but you could add some chopped, cooked chicken breasts or cannelloni beans to increase the protein. This is wonderful served over polenta, but you can also serve it over rice, or simply by itself.

1 large eggplant, peeled and cut into 1-inch cubes

2 teaspoons salt

3 tablespoons olive oil

1 large red onion, chopped

4 medium-size zucchini, cut into ¼ -inch-thick chunks

1 large red bell pepper, chopped

1 large yellow bell pepper, chopped

10 cloves garlic, chopped

1 cup mushrooms, sliced

2 (15-ounce) cans stewed tomatoes

¼ cup red wine

1 cup fresh basil, chopped

1 cup chopped fresh parsley

½ teaspoon freshly ground pepper, or to taste

1 bay leaf

- Sprinkle the eggplant cubes with 1 teaspoon of the salt and set on paper towels to absorb liquid for 20 minutes, turning after 10 minutes. Rinse and pat dry.
- In a large Dutch oven, combine the olive oil and onion, and sauté for 4 to 5 minutes, or until soft. Add the zucchini, peppers, garlic, mushrooms, and eggplant, and sauté for another 8 to 10 minutes. Add the tomatoes, red wine, basil, bay leaf, and parsley. Simmer over medium-low heat for 30 minutes. Add the freshly ground pepper and a teaspoon of salt, and cover. Simmer until veggies are cooked through, about 1 hour

nutritional analysis per serving
277.25 calories; 15.94 g fat (52% calories from fat); 24.73 g protein; 8.31 g carbohydrate; 555.32 mg cholesterol; 381.70 mg sodium

Red Curry Seafood

PREP/COOK TIME: 30 minutes
SERVE: Serves 6

I like adding calamari to this dish. This recipe reminds me of my favorite Asian restaurant—the smells as it cooks, the warmth of the curry—it's just delightful.

¼ cup brown rice flour

Salt and pepper

1 pound jumbo shrimp, fresh if possible

3 tablespoons olive oil

1 small zucchini, sliced

1 small red onion, chopped

3 cloves garlic, minced

1 small red bell pepper, sliced

1 cup bok choy, chopped

1 cup napa cabbage, chopped

2 large carrots, chopped

¼ pound fresh green beans

1 (12-ounce) can light coconut milk

½ tablespoon red curry paste

- Combine the flour, salt, and pepper, seasoning to taste.
- Clean and devein the shrimp and dredge in the flour mixture. Heat a large skillet, and heat 2 tablespoons of the olive oil. Add the shrimp and cook on high to sear in the juices. Cook for 1 to 2 minutes on each side. Remove from the heat and set aside. Add 1 tablespoon of the olive oil and the vegetables to the skillet and stir-fry until crisp-tender, 8 to 10 minutes. Reduce the heat and simmer for a minute or two.
- In small skillet, combine the coconut milk and red curry paste. Stir and cook until it comes to a boil. Reduce the heat and continue to cook for about 5 minutes. Combine the coconut mixture with the shrimp mixture and heat through.
- I serve this dish over red rice, but any rice is fine.

nutritional analysis per serving
332.12 calories; 21.88 g fat (55% calories from fat); 20.00 g protein; 17.07 g carbohydrate; 114.91 mg cholesterol; 940.16 mg sodium

Roast Leg of Lamb
with Caper Sauce

PREP TIME: 10 minutes to prepare; roasting times vary
SERVE: Serves 8

If you like garlic, try making a few slits in the leg before roasting, and slip a half clove of garlic into each slit. Be sure to test for doneness with a meat thermometer. If you don't like capers, you can serve this with mint sauce, or try the Peach Salsa on page 190.

1 (2-pound) leg of lamb
2 tablespoons olive oil
2 tablespoons chopped parsley
1 teaspoon fresh rosemary
½ teaspoon salt
Freshly cracked pepper, to taste
1 recipe Caper Sauce (page 188)

- Preheatthe oven to 325°F.
- Rinse the lamb and pat dry. Baste with the olive oil and sprinkle on the herbs, salt, and pepper. Bake until the lamb reaches 175°–180°F.

nutritional analysis per serving
231.35 calories; 15.32 g fat (60% calories from fat); 21.23 g protein; 0.74 g carbohydrate; 75.98 mg cholesterol; 210.88 mg sodium

Roast Pork Tenderloins

PREP TIME: 10 minutes to prepare and 20 minutes to bake

SERVE: Serves 6

My main taste tester, Daniel, loved this recipe. I've made this dish with the nectarines as directed, but I have also made it with peaches and it's just as good.

2 pears, quartered

5 dried nectarines or peaches

2 tablespoons olive oil

3 tablespoons fresh sage, chopped, or herbes de Provence

2 pounds pork tenderloins

4 cloves garlic, peeled and sliced in half

1 teaspoon salt

1 teaspoon pepper

■ In a large bowl combine the pears, nectarines, olive oil, and 2 tablespoons of the sage. Stir until well blended. Set aside.

■ Heat the oven to 500°F. Prepare the tenderloins by cutting four slits in each tenderloin and stuffing half a clove of garlic into each slit. Sprinkle salt and pepper over the meat and rub with 1 tablespoon of the sage.

■ Place the tenderloins in a large roasting pan, arrange the fruit around the meat, and pour the olive oil over the top. Sprinkle in the herbs. Bake for 20 minutes in total, turning the meat and fruit halfway through. Be sure to coat the fruit with juices from the roasting pan.

nutritional analysis per serving
345.08 calories; 13.63 g fat (35% calories from fat); 34.10 g protein; 22.01 g carbohydrate; 89.21 mg cholesterol; 273.71 mg sodium

Salmon with Miso

PREP TIME: 2 hours to prepare and 15 minutes to cook
SERVES: Serves 4

This salmon is wonderful as is, or served over a bed of lightly steamed spinach. For a richer meal, serve over mashed potatoes, pouring the sauce over the top before serving. Top with chopped green onions, if desired.

- 2 tablespoons brown rice syrup
- 2 tablespoons lemon juice
- 1 cup miso
- 1 teaspoon peeled and grated fresh ginger
- 3 cloves garlic, minced
- 1 pound salmon fillet
- 2 green onions, chopped (optional)

- Place the brown rice syrup, lemon juice, miso, ginger, and garlic in a food processor or blender and puree until smooth.
- Lay the salmon fillet in a flat baking dish and cover with the miso sauce. Place in the refrigerator for 1 to 2 hours. Remove the fish from the miso sauce. Reserve sauce. Preheat the grill and cook the salmon for 6 to 7 minutes on each side, or until done. Heat the reserved miso sauce and pour over the grilled salmon.

nutritional analysis per serving
334.96 calories; 9.09 g fat (24% calories from fat);
29.53 g protein; 36.21 g carbohydrate; 26.08 mg cholesterol, 360 mg sodium

Salsa Chicken

PREP TIME: 10 minutes to prepare and about 30 minutes to cook
SERVES: 6

This is an easy meal to prepare. For a complete meal, add a salad and the Mexican Cornbread found on page 35. This chicken is also quite nice served over a bed of quinoa.

1 cup salsa (see box)
¼ cup water
2 cloves garlic, minced
1 tablespoon olive oil
4 chicken breasts, skinned
Salt and pepper

- Combine the salsa (see below) and water in a small bowl and set aside.
- In a large skillet, sauté the garlic in olive oil over medium heat for 1 to 2 minutes. Add the chicken breasts and cook on each side for 5 minutes.
- Add the salsa mixture, salt, and pepper to the skillet. Turn heat to medium-low and cover. Simmer for 20 minutes, or until the chicken is tender.

Salsa Recipe
   PREP TIME: 10 minutes

½ cup fresh tomatoes, chopped
½ cup red onion, chopped
1 tablespoon finely chopped cilantro
¼ teaspoon ground cumin
¼ teaspoon salt
Freshly ground black pepper, to taste

In a large bowl, mix together all the ingredients.

---

nutritional analysis per serving
524.43 calories; 9.24 g fat (15% calories from fat); 48.08 g protein; 61.59 g carbohydrate; 91.25 mg cholesterol; 333.73 mg sodium

Sea Bass with Basil

PREP TIME: 20 minutes
SERVES: 4

This is a wonderful fish dish, high in protein, low in carbs, and full of flavor. You can use other white fish in place of the sea bass, such as cod or snapper. Feel free to use whatever is native to your region. Grilling will vary depending on the thickness of the fish.

¼ cup fresh basil

2 cloves garlic

3 tablespoons grated Parmesan cheese

2 tablespoons olive oil

4 (4-ounce) sea bass fillets

¼ teaspoon pepper

- Preheat the grill (or you can also sauté the fish on the stove).
- Place the basil, garlic, Parmesan cheese, and olive oil in a blender and process until smooth. If the mixture is too thick, thin it with either water, soup stock, or a touch of wine.
- Grill the fish for 5 to 8 minutes on each side, or until done, sprinkle with pepper, and serve with the basil pesto on the side.

nutritional analysis per serving
214.83 calories; 10.59 g fat (44% calories from fat); 25.97 g protein; 3.48 g carbohydrate; 0 mg cholesterol; 437.26 mg sodium

Shrimp Curry

NO DAIRY, EGGS, OR NUTS

PREP TIME: 20 to 30 minutes
SERVES: 6

I suggest you serve this over rice noodles but, for a change, why not serve it over roasted spaghetti squash? Spaghetti squash is a very low-calorie squash. A 4-ounce serving only yields 37 calories. It stores for about a month in a cool place, and is available year round. To prepare it, pierce in all over several times with a fork and bake in a 375°F oven for about an hour, or until the flesh is soft. Cut open and scoop out the spaghetti-like pulp and place in a large bowl. Add the shrimp curry and toss. You'll love it.

2 tablespoons olive oil

1 large red onion, chopped finely

1 large red bell pepper, sliced thinly

1 tablespoon peeled and grated fresh ginger

4 cloves garlic, minced

1 cup chopped napa cabbage

½ pound baby bok choy, chopped

14 ounces light coconut milk

2 teaspoons red curry paste

2 tablespoons Asian fish sauce

½ pound medium-size shrimp, washed and deveined

1 tablespoon oil

8 ounces rice noodles

- In a large skillet, heat the oil and sauté the onion until soft, about 5 minutes. Add the red bell pepper, ginger, and garlic. Continue to cook, stirring occasionally, for 2 minutes. Add the cabbage and bok choy, and sauté until soft, 2 to 3 minutes.

- In a small pan, heat the coconut milk. Add the red curry paste and the fish sauce. Stir to combine well. Add to the vegetables and heat until mixture thickens. Set aside.

- In a small saucepan, sauté the shrimp in 1 tablespoon of oil until cooked, 1 to 2 minutes on each side. Add to the vegetable mixture.

- Cook the rice noodles according to the package directions and drain. Place in a large bowl. Add the shrimp mixture and toss well. Serve immediately.

nutritional analysis per serving

284.10 calories; 20.39 g fat (61% calories from fat); 10.84 g protein; 17.11 g carbohydrate; 57.46 mg cholesterol; 102.33 mg sodium

Shrimp Frittata

PREP/COOK TIME: 45 minutes
SERVES: 4

What I like about the frittata is there is no crust, so it's easy to make, contains far less calories than quiche, and takes less time. If you don't like shrimp, replace it with a meat of your choice or tofu.

1 tablespoon olive oil

1 large onion, chopped finely

1 medium-size red bell pepper, chopped

1 small zucchini, sliced

3 cloves garlic, chopped

8 eggs

½ cup choppedparsley

1 large tomato, chopped

6 ounces shrimp, peeled, washed, and deveined

¼ teaspoon salt

¼ teaspoon pepper

- Preheat the oven to 350°F.
- In a 10-inch ovenproof skillet, heat the oil and add the onion. Sauté until soft, 3 to 4 minutes. Add the bell pepper, zucchini, and garlic. Sauté for 2 minutes.
- In a separate bowl, beat the eggs. Slowly add to the vegetable mixture. Add the parsley and tomato. Arrange the shrimp on top, and sprinkle with salt and pepper. Place in the preheated oven and bake until set, 10 to 15 minutes.
- Serve warm.

nutritional analysis per serving
277.25 calories; 15.94 g fat (52% calories from fat); 24.73 g protein; 8.31 g carbohydrate; 555.32 mg cholesterol; 381.70 mg sodium

Shrimp Jambalaya

PREP TIME: 15 minutes to prepare and 30 to 40 minutes to cook

SERVES: 8

Be sure to use long-grain rice in this recipe. If you use a heartier rice such as short-grain brown rice, you will need to increase the cooking time, as it will take longer to cook. This recipe is a full meal, and is great leftover for lunch or another meal.

2 tablespoons extra-virgin olive oil

1 large onion, chopped finely

1 large red bell pepper, chopped

½ large green bell pepper, chopped

½ cup celery, chopped

1 small leek, chopped

1 (10-ounce) can diced green chiles

½ pound fresh mushrooms, cleaned and sliced

5 cloves garlic, chopped

4 cups vegetable broth

1½ cups long-grain brown rice

1 tablespoon chopped fresh parsley

½ teaspoon dried thyme

1 (14½-ounce) stewed tomatoes with oregano and basil

1 pound medium-size shrimp, washed, peeled, and deveined

■ Sauté the onion, peppers, celery, leeks, chiles, and mushrooms in a Dutch oven over medium-high heat for 7 minutes, or until the vegetables are soft. Add the garlic and cook another 2 minutes. Add the vegetable broth, rice, herbs, and tomatoes. Bring to a boil and then reduce the heat to low. Cover and cook until the rice is tender, about 30 minutes. Add the shrimp and heat through.

nutritional analysis per serving

268.68 calories; 7.01 g fat (23% calories from fat); 18.25 g protein; 33.81 g carbohydrate; 87.41 mg cholesterol; 1179.89 mg sodium

Spinach and Mushroom Quiche

PREP TIME: 15 minutes to prepare and 40 to 45 minutes to bake
SERVES: 6

This quiche is great for breakfast, lunch, or dinner. I don't think it will last long in your house, but it sure is good as leftovers. This makes a great meal to take to a brunch during the holidays. You can also make this recipe using swiss chard—it's delightful.

4 cups fresh spinach, washed (or 10 ounces frozen)

2 tablespoons olive oil

½ cup red onion, chopped fine

2 cloves garlic, chopped fine

1 cup mushrooms, sliced

pastry dough (see page 223)

½ cup cottage cheese

1 cup Swiss cheese, grated

2 large eggs, beaten

1 cup milk

¼ teaspoon grated nutmeg

½ teaspoon salt

¼ teaspoon pepper

- Preheat the oven to 350°F.
- Steam the spinach until it wilts, about 5 minutes. Drain well and let cool. Be sure to squeeze out the excess liquid from the spinach, then chop coarsely.
- In a medium-size skillet, heat the oil and sauté the onion until soft. Add the garlic and mushrooms, and continue cooking for 2 to 3 minutes. Add the spinach and mix well. Roll out your pastry dough and place it carefully in a greased pie plate. Spread the cottage cheese over the pastry. Next, spread the spinach mixture over the cottage cheese, then spread the Swiss cheese over the top.
- In a small bowl, beat the eggs and combine with the milk, nutmeg, salt, and pepper. Pour over the spinach and cheese, and bake for 40 to 45 minutes. Oven temperatures vary, so check the quiche at 35 minutes. If it is set, remove from the oven. Otherwise, continue baking until the quiche is set and lightly browned.

> This delicious quiche can be made ahead and stored in the refrigerator.

nutritional analysis per serving
191.90 calories; 13.42 g fat (62% calories from fat); 12.49 g protein; 5.51 g carbohydrate; 92.25 mg cholesterol; 362.41 mg sodium

Stir-fried Veggies
with Tomato Pesto

PREP/COOK TIME: 30 minutes
SERVES: 4

This is a *great stir-fry, but by itself it lacks protein. You can add tofu, chicken, or beef to increase the amount of protein or serve it along side the Sweet-and-Sour Chicken on page 127 or the Beef and Broccoli stir-fry on page 84.*

2 tablespoons olive oil

1 small onion, sliced finely

¼ pound baby carrots, chopped

1 small red bell pepper, sliced finely

3 cloves garlic, minced

1 small zucchini, sliced

½ pound fresh green beans, steamed, cut in half

4 leaves napa cabbage, chopped

1 tablespoon tomato pesto (see below)

Salt and pepper, to taste

Tomato Pesto:

⅓ cup sun-dried tomatoes, drained and softened in water

3–4 cloves garlic, minced

¼ cup olive oil (more if too dry)

½ cup chopped fresh basil leaves

¼ cup chopped fresh parsley

¼ cup grated Parmesan cheese

■ Heat the olive oil in a large skillet. Sauté the onions, carrots, and red bell pepper over medium-high heat for 4 to 5 minutes, then add the garlic, zucchini, green beans, and cabbage. Continue cooking until the veggies begin to brown and are cooked through. Meanwhile, place all the pesto ingredients in a blender and puree until smooth. Lower the heat and add the tomato pesto, salt, and pepper.

■ I serve this dish over red rice, but if you don't have red rice, serve over any rice you prefer.

nutritional analysis per serving

133.53 calories; 8.93 g fat (59% calories from fat); 3.51 g protein; 12.27 g carbohydrate; 1.08 mg cholesterol; 104.37 mg sodium

Stuffed Bell Peppers

PREP TIME: 15 minutes to prepare and about 45 minutes to cook and bake
SERVES: 4

If you don't have any pine nuts on hand, try substituting walnuts or pecans. You can leave the nuts out altogether if you prefer, but they really do add a nice crunch and flavor to the dish.

½ cup cooked basmati rice

2 tablespoons olive oil

1 large red onion, chopped finely

2 cloves garlic, minced

3 large bell peppers (red, green or yellow)

½ pound Roma tomatoes, peeled and chopped

5 sun-dried tomatoes, chopped

1 teaspoon ground cumin

½ teaspoon groundallspice

½ teaspoon chile powder

3 tablespoons chopped parsley

⅔ cup pine nuts

- Preheat the oven to 350°F.
- Cook the rice according to the directions on the packaging. Set aside.
- Heat a large skillet over medium heat and sauté the onion until soft, about 5 minutes. Add the garlic and sauté for an additional 3 minutes.
- Cut each pepper in half and scoop out the seeds. Set aside. Meanwhile, add the fresh and dried tomatoes to the onions and garlic, and sauté for 1 minute. Add the spices and parsley, and cook for 2 minutes. Stir in the pine nuts and cooked rice, then stuff the peppers with this mixture.
- Pour water into the bottom of an 8-inch square baking pan and place the peppers bottom side down. Cover with foil and bake for 30 minutes.
- Uncover and bake another 15 minutes. Serve warm.

nutritional analysis per serving
278.23 calories; 22.98 g fat (70% calories from fat); 5.72 g protein; 17.75 g carbohydrate; 0 mg cholesterol; 65.41 mg sodium

Stuffed Winter Squash

NO EGGS

PREP TIME: 30 minutes to prepare and 20 minutes to bake
SERVES: 4

Years ago I visited Moosewood Restaurant in Ithaca, New York. I love all the Moosewood cookbooks, and was thrilled to eat dinner in their restaurant. I had a stuffed winter squash there that knocked my socks off. I couldn't wait to come home and try to make something similar. This is as close as I could get, and I just love it. I hope you do, too.

2 medium-size butternut squash

Water as needed

1 large onion, chopped finely

1 large red bell pepper, chopped finely

1 large apple, chopped finely

2 tablespoons olive oil

3 cloves garlic, minced

1 teaspoon fresh rosemary

¼ cup freshly grated Parmesan cheese

½ cup walnuts or pecans, chopped coarsely

½ teaspoon salt

¼ teaspoon freshly ground pepper

- Preheat the oven to 350°F.
- Slice the squash in half and scoop out the seeds. Place the squash, cut side down, in a baking pan and add enough water to cover the bottom of the pan. Bake at 350°F for 30 to 40 minutes, or until the squash is soft to the touch. Remove from the oven and set aside.
- In a large skillet, sauté the chopped onion, red bell pepper, and apple in the oil for 4 to 5 minutes. Add the garlic and rosemary, and continue to sauté for 1 minute.
- Scoop out the insides of the squash (but keep the shells), add to the onion mixture, and sauté for 1 to 2 minutes. Remove from the heat and add the Parmesan cheese and walnuts.
- Lay the squash shells skin side down on a baking sheet and carefully stuff the vegetable mixture into each half of the squash. Sprinkle with the salt and pepper. Bake at 350°F for 20 minutes, or until heated through.

nutritional analysis per serving
159.47 calories; 9.76 g fat (51% calories from fat); 3.52 g protein; 18.25 g carbohydrate; 50 mg cholesterol; 295.47 mg sodium

Sun-dried Tomato Meat Loaf

PREP TIME: 30 minutes to prepare and about 1 hour to bake
SERVES: 8

This is a wonderful base for a meat loaf, but you can certainly add to it. I have added kalamata olives, a dash of red wine, or cornflakes in place of the millet or rice cereal. I usually make it with the bison, but it can be made with beef or turkey, too.

1 cup sun-dried tomatoes

2 cups boiling water

¼ cup rice or millet cereal, crushed

1 large onion, chopped

½ medium-size green bell pepper, chopped

1 tablespoon olive oil

4 cloves garlic, minced

2 tablespoons mushroom or vegetable broth

2 large eggs

½ cup creamy havarti cheese, shredded

2 teaspoons dried basil

1 teaspoon dried parsley

1 teaspoon dried oregano

½ teaspoon dried thyme

½ teaspoon freshly ground pepper

½ teaspoon salt

1½ pounds ground turkey, beef, or buffalo

vegetable oil spray

- Preheat the oven to 350°F.
- Soften the tomatoes in the boiling water and then drain. Chop and place in a large bowl. Add the crushed cereal and mix to coat. Set aside.
- Sauté the onion and green pepper in the olive oil until soft, about 5 to 6 minutes. Add the garlic and sauté for another minute. Add to the tomato mixture, then the broth. Beat the eggs and add to the mixture. Mix well. Add the cheese, herbs, seasonings, and meat. Stir until well blended.
- Press the mixture into a 9 × 5-inch loaf pan lightly coated with vegetable oil spray. Bake for 1 hour, or until the temperature of the loaf, when measured with a roasting thermometer, reaches 170°F.
- Remove from the oven and let cool for 5 to 10 minutes before removing from the loaf pan. Cut into slices and serve warm.

nutritional analysis per serving
303.06 calories; 21.23 g fat (62% calories from fat); 21.07 g protein; 7.04 g carbohydrate; 121.49 mg cholesterol; 308.08 mg sodium

Sweet-and-Sour Chicken

PREP TIME: 10 minutes to prepare and up to 1½ hours to bake
SERVES: 6

Serve this with *the Stir-fried Veggies found on page 123 and you have a great meal.*

½ cup wheat-free tamari sauce
¾ cup fruit sweetened ketchup
¼ cup agave nectar
3 cloves garlic, minced
1 teaspoon prepared mustard
1 fryer chicken, cut into pieces

- Preheat the oven to 350°F.
- Combine all ingredients except the chicken in a small bowl and stir until well blended.
- Place the chicken sections in a 9 × 13-inch baking dish. Cover with the sauce and bake for 1 to 1½ hours, or until done.

nutritional analysis per serving
121.04 calories; 0.73 g fat (5% of calories from fat); 12.28 g protein; 19.05 g carbohydrate; 22.81 mg cholesterol; 1711.23 mg sodium

Vegetable Frittata

PREP/COOK TIME: 45 to 50 minutes
SERVE: Serves 6

This can be served for breakfast, brunch, or dinner. It is beautiful and chock full of complex carbohydrates and protein. It tastes great and should be served hot.

2 tablespoons olive oil

1 cup red onions, sliced thinly

1 cup red potatoes, sliced thinly

1 cup yams, sliced thinly

1 small zucchini, sliced thinly

1 cup chopped spinach

1 large red bell pepper, chopped

3 cloves garlic, chopped

4 large eggs

8 egg whites

1 teaspoon dried oregano

1 tablespoon dried parsley

½ teaspoon salt

4 ounces Swiss cheese, grated

¼ teaspoon freshly ground pepper

½ cup chopped fresh tomatoes

■ In a 10-inch skillet, heat the olive oil and sauté the onion until soft, 4 to 5 minutes. Add the potatoes and yams and continue cooking, covered, for 8 to 10 minutes, or until the potatoes are tender. Add the zucchini, spinach, red bell pepper and garlic. Cook for 3 minutes. Set aside the skillet. Turn off heat.

■ In a large bowl, combine the eggs, egg whites, herbs and salt. Pour over the vegetable mixture and stir to mix well. Cook over low heat until the eggs begin to set, about 10 minutes. Place the chopped tomatoes on top. Sprinkle the Swiss cheese and freshly ground pepper over the top. Cover and cook until the cheese is melted and the eggs are set.

nutritional analysis per serving
250.23 calories; 13.41 g fat (47% calories from fat); 15.89 g protein; 16.75 g carbohydrate; 158.39 mg cholesterol; 363.90 mg sodium

pasta, rice, and beans

Artichoke Heart Risotto

PREP/COOK TIME: 35 to 45 minutes
SERVE: Serves 6

I love risotto, and this version is quite good. I recommend you use Italian kalamata olives in this recipe to enhance the flavors. If you wish to add some cheese, fresh grated Parmesan is best.

2 tablespoons olive oil

1 large red onion, chopped

1 large red bell pepper, chopped

4 cloves garlic, minced

1 (12-ounce) can artichoke hearts, drained, chopped

½ teaspoon dried rosemary

¼ cup fresh parsley

2 cups arborio rice

1 quart mushroom or chicken broth

½ cup olives, pitted and sliced

½ teaspoon salt

¼ teaspoon ground pepper

- In a Dutch oven or large skillet, heat the olive oil over medium heat. Add the red onion and sauté 4 to 5 minutes. Add the bell pepper, garlic, and artichoke hearts. Continue to sauté for 2 to 3 minutes more. Add the rosemary, parsley, and rice. Stir to mix all ingredients.

- In a separate saucepan, heat the mushroom broth to a boil. Slowly add, a ladleful at a time, to the rice mixture, stirring constantly and making sure all of the liquid is absorbed before adding more. Continue this process until all of the broth has been added and the rice mixture is cooked through. Add the olives, and salt and pepper, to taste. Serve immediately.

nutritional analysis per serving
383.66 calories; 10.10 g fat (23% calories from fat); 7.75 g protein; 64.76 g carbohydrate; 0 mg cholesterol; 1051 mg sodium

Bean and Mushroom Chili

PREP TIME: 15 minutes preparation and 1 hour cooking time
SERVE: Serves 8 to 10

If you are looking for a high-protein meal this is it. The combination of the black beans and cannellini beans with the mushrooms is delightful. The mustard seeds really add a unique flavor to this dish. Feel free to adjust the amount of mustard to suit your taste. I like additional cilantro as a garnish. You can also add a dollop of guacamole on top.

1 tablespoon extra-virgin olive oil

1–2 tablespoons mustard seeds

1 tablespoon chile powder

1½ teaspoons cumin seeds or ground cumin

½ teaspoon ground cardamom

1 large onion, chopped

3 cloves garlic, chopped

¾ pound mushrooms, cleaned and sliced

½ cup water

1 (14-ounce) can organic black beans, drained

1 (14½-ounce) can cannellini beans (white kidney beans), drained

3 cups mushroom or chicken broth

1 (6-ounce) can tomato paste

½ cup fresh cilantro

- Heat the olive oil in a Dutch oven over medium-high heat. Add the mustard seeds, chile powder, cumin, and cardamom. Stir constantly until the seeds start to pop. Add the onion, garlic, mushrooms, and water. Reduce the heat and cook for 10 minutes, covered. Uncover and continue cooking until the liquid is absorbed and veggies are lightly browned, stirring frequently. Add the beans, mushroom broth, and tomato paste, and stir to blend well. Add the cilantro and cook over low heat until heated through—about 1 hour.

- This is wonderful served with yogurt and additional cilantro.

nutritional analysis per serving
323.13 calories; 5.33 g fat (14% calories from fat); 19.64 g protein; 52.72 g carbohydrate; 0 mg cholesterol; 658.96 mg sodium

Bean and Quinoa Chili

PREP/COOK TIME: 60 to 70 minutes
SERVE: Serves 8

Quinoa is a light and fluffy seed, usually called a grain. It adapts well in most recipes and adds a nice texture to this recipe.

1 cup quinoa, rinsed and drained

2 cups water

1 tablespoon vegetable oil

1 large onion, diced

1 large green bell pepper, chopped finely

1 large red bell pepper, chopped finely

1 cup diced carrots

1 jalapeño pepper, seeded and chopped finely

2 (14-ounce) cans kidney beans, drained

1 (28-ounce) can crushed tomatoes

1 tablespoon chile powder

1 teaspoon dried oregano

2 teaspoons ground cumin

½ teaspoon salt

¼ teaspoon ground pepper

■ Combine the quinoa and water in a saucepan. Cover and bring to a boil over medium-high heat. Lower the heat and cook until the liquid is absorbed and the quinoa is light and fluffy, about 15 minutes. Remove from the heat and let stand 10 minutes.

■ Meanwhile, heat the oil in a large skillet and add the onion, bell peppers, carrots, and jalapeño. Sauté for 5 to 6 minutes over medium heat. Stir in the beans, crushed tomatoes, and herbs. Cook for about 30 minutes over low heat. Add the quinoa and heat through. Season with salt and pepper.

nutritional analysis per serving
228.51 calories; 2.82 g fat (8% calories from fat);
11.11 g protein; 43.29 g carbohydrate; 0 mg cholesterol;
614.87 mg sodium

Bean Burgers

NO DAIRY OR NUTS

PREP TIME: 10 minutes to prepare and 10 to 15 minutes to cook
SERVE: Serves 4 (2 patties per serving)

These burgers can be served on top of a large sliced tomato and a bed of lettuce, or with a salad and a vegetable for a quick, easy meal. For an egg-free patty, combine 3 tablespoons of water with 1 tablespoon of ground flaxseeds. Blend together until thick, and add to the mixture.

½ cup zucchini

1 cup mushrooms

2 cloves garlic

½ small onion

1 egg

2 tablespoons olive oil

1 teaspoon dried basil

1 teaspoon driedoregano

½ teaspoon dried parsley

1 cup garbanzo bean flour

½ teaspoon salt

¼ teaspoon ground pepper

1 tablespoon vegetable oil, for frying

- Finely chop the zucchini, mushrooms, garlic, and onion. Place in a large bowl. Add the egg, olive oil, herbs, garbanzo flour, salt, and pepper. Mix until well blended.

- In a large skillet, heat the vegetable oil over medium-high heat. With a large spoon, scoop out the batter and drop onto the skillet to form four to six patties about ½-inch thick. Lower the temperature to medium after they start to brown, and cook slowly. They should cook about 5 minutes on each side.

nutritional analysis per serving
141.39 calories; 11.86 g fat (74% calories from fat); 3.11 g protein; 6.46 g carbohydrate; 61.33 mg cholesterol; 314.52 mg sodium

Bean Enchiladas

PREP TIME: 20 minutes to prepare and about 20 minutes to cook
SERVE: Serves 4

Corn tortillas often break while rolling up with fillings. So why not try the crêpe recipe in place of the tortillas? They won't have an affect on the flavor, and will help you keep the burritos intact while you eat them.

1 cup cooked kidney beans

1 cup cooked black beans

1 small onion, chopped

2 cloves garlic, minced

2 tablespoons olive oil

1 tablespoon chile powder

1 teaspoon cumin

1 tablespoon lime juice

8 corn tortillas

3 cups salsa

½ cup cheddar cheese, shredded (optional)

- Preheat the oven to 350°F.
- Mash the beans in a bowl until smooth.
- Sauté the onion and garlic in oil until they begin to brown. Add the spices, lime juice, and beans. Heat through.
- Soften the corn tortillas by wrapping them in a damp towel and placing in the microwave for 30 seconds. You can also soften tortillas in a skillet over a mid-to-low heat. Place about ⅓ cup of the bean mixture and a small amount of cheese on each tortilla and roll up. Place seam side down in a casserole dish and cover with salsa. Sprinkle with the remaining cheese. Bake for 15 to 20 minutes, or until the sauce begins to bubble and the cheese is melted.

> You can use nondairy Cheddar cheese if you prefer.

nutritional analysis per serving
439.92 calories; 14.98 g fat (30% calories from fat); 17.71 g protein; 64.38 g carbohydrate; 17.33 mg cholesterol; 1195.73 mg sodium

Black Bean Burritos

PREP TIME: 30 minutes to prepare, from start to finish
SERVE: Serves 4

These are my son Rory's favorite burritos. We like them with lots of cilantro and lime, but you can always cut it down to suit your taste. We've also used yogurt in place of the sour cream, and love to make homemade guacamole to go with this meal.

This only makes enough for 4 people; if you want leftovers you really should double the recipe. Be sure to soften the tortillas in a towel in the oven or use the crêpes found on page 214.

1 tablespoon olive oil

1 cup chopped red onion

½ cup chopped green bell pepper

¾ cup chopped red bell pepper

2 tablespoons finely chopped jalapeño pepper

2 cloves garlic, minced

1 (15-ounce) can black beans, drained and mashed

½ cup corn, fresh or frozen

3 tablespoons chopped cilantro

3 tablespoons lime juice, fresh if possible

1½ teaspoons chile powder

¼ teaspoon salt

1 teaspoon ground cumin

Dash of red pepper flakes

4 corn tortillas (softened)

1½ cups Monterey Jack cheese, shredded

½ cup salsa

¼ cup sour cream (optional)

- Preheat the oven to 350°F.
- Heat the olive oil in a large skillet or Dutch oven and add the onion. Sauté over medium heat for 3 to 4 minutes, or until soft, then add the green bell pepper, red bell pepper, jalapeño pepper, and garlic; continue sautéing for 3 minutes, or until vegetables are tender. Add the beans, corn, cilantro, lime juice, chile powder, salt, cumin, and red pepper flakes. Remove from the heat and set aside. Place the corn tortillas in a moist towel and place in the microwave for a few seconds, or soften by steaming on the stove in a pan with a small amount of water.
- Spoon half a cup of the bean mixture across the center of each softened tortilla. Top each with 2 to 4 tablespoons of cheese, and roll up. Place burritos seam side down in a greased 9-inch square baking dish. Sprinkle a small amount of cheese on top and bake for 15 to 20 minutes, or until heated all the way through. Serve with salsa and sour cream, if desired.

nutritional analysis per serving
482.93 calories; 20.87 g fat (38% calories from fat); 23.41 g protein; 62.09 g carbohydrate; 44.06 mg cholesterol; 767.36 mg sodium

Creamy Pesto Pasta

PREP/COOK TIME: 20 minutes
SERVE: Serves 6

Spaghetti squash is a great alternative to traditional pasta. I like lentil pasta, too, as is higher in protein and provides a richer flavor, but it is hard to find. Ask your local grocer or health food store to order it for you. You won't be disappointed.

8 ounces rice noodles
1 large red onion, finely chopped
5 cloves garlic, minced
1 tablespoon olive oil
8 ounces Neufchâtel cheese
¾ cup chicken broth
¼ cup dry white wine
1 cup chopped fresh basil
Salt
Pepper
Parmesan cheese (optional)

- Cook the noodles according to the package directions. Drain.
- In a large skillet, sauté the onion and garlic in the olive oil until soft, about 4 to 5 minutes. Add the cheese and lower the heat. Stir until the cheese melts. Do not let this mixture come to a boil or burn. Stir in the chicken broth, wine, and basil. Stir until the mixture is well blended and the basil is wilted. Add water if it is too thick.
- Pour over the rice noodles and season with salt and pepper to taste. Sprinkle with Parmesan cheese, if desired.

Try this recipe using spaghetti squash.

nutritional analysis per serving
196.35 calories; 10.35 g fat (46% of calories from fat); 6.72 g protein; 20.04 g carbohydrate; 28.73 mg cholesterol; 258.77 mg sodium

Indian-Style Lentils

PREP/COOK TIME: 1 hour. Can be made ahead and stored in the refrigerator
SERVE: Serves 6

You'll love the coconut milk in this recipe. This dish will warm you from the inside out. Add more vegetables if you wish; cauliflower works well. Serve as a side dish, or for lunch as the main dish with a salad on the side.

2 teaspoons mustard seeds

4 tablespoons olive oil

1 onion, chopped finely

3 cloves garlic, minced

1 tablespoon peeled and grated fresh ginger

1 teaspoon ground turmeric

1 cup red or yellow lentils

4 cups water

1¼ cups light coconut milk

½–1 teaspoon salt

Freshly ground pepper, to taste

■ In a large skillet, heat the mustard seeds in the oil. Cook until the seeds begin to pop; add the onion. Continue cooking until the onion is soft, 4 to 5 minutes. Add the garlic and ginger, and continue cooking for 2 minutes. Add the turmeric and stir.

■ Add the lentils and cook, stirring frequently, until the lentils begin to turn translucent, about 3 minutes.

■ Add the water, coconut milk, salt, and pepper. Stir well. Bring to boil, then reduce the heat and simmer 45 minutes, until done.

nutritional analysis per serving
337.64 calories; 22.76 g fat (58% calories from fat); 10.45 g protein; 26.53 g carbohydrate; 0 mg cholesterol; 402.27 mg sodium

Lentil Patties with Spinach

NO DAIRY OR EGGS (CONTAINS PEANUT OIL)

PREP/COOK TIME: 30 minutes (not including soaking time)
SERVE: Serves 4

These patties are a great source of protein, and a wonderful lunch or snack food. You can store them in the refrigerator for several days, and they taste great with a dollop of hummus or peanut sauce on top.

¾ cup red or pink lentils, washed

3 tablespoons vegetable stock, plus more if needed

3 cups spinach, chopped

1 small serrano chile

2 tablespoons leeks, chopped finely

1 clove garlic

½ teaspoon salt

1 tablespoon chopped cilantro

2 teaspoons brown rice flour

3 tablespoons peanut oil

- Soak the lentils overnight in water. Drain and puree in a blender with the vegetable stock until smooth.
- In a large bowl, combine all of the ingredients except the peanut oil; mix well.
- Heat a large skillet over medium-high heat and pour in a tablespoon of peanut oil. Drop a tablespoon of the mixture onto the skillet and flatten it with the back of a spoon. Do this with as many patties as you can fit into the skillet. Cook for 2 minutes on each side, or until browned. Remove from the heat and place on a dish. Repeat with remaining lentil mixture, heating extra oil between batches as necessary.

nutritional analysis per serving
54.00 calories; 5.90 g fat (34% calories from fat); 5.24 g protein; 20.65 g carbohydrate; 0.06 mg cholesterol; 196.83 mg sodium

Mushroom Risotto

PREP/COOK TIME: 35 to 45 minutes
SERVE: Serves 6

Oh boy do I love this recipe. I highly recommend you use wild mushrooms in this recipe, such as chanterelles. It will really enhance the flavors. This takes some time, as you have to keep stirring the rice as it cooks, but it's worth it.

1 pound mushrooms, sliced

4 tablespoons olive oil

4 cloves garlic, minced

3 tablespoons chopped parsley

1 small onion, chopped

¾ cup arborio rice

6 cups vegetable broth, heated to boiling

6 ounces Swiss cheese, grated

1 tablespoon tarragon, fresh if possible

Salt and pepper, to taste

- Sauté the mushrooms in 1 tablespoon of the oil. Add the garlic and parsley once the juices from the mushrooms begin to run. Remove from the heat and cover. Set aside.
- In a large skillet, sauté the onion in the rest of the oil over medium heat. Add the rice and stir until it is coated with the oil and begins to pop. Add a ladleful of the hot vegetable broth and stir the mixture until all of the liquid is absorbed. Add another ladleful of broth, and continue this process until all of the broth has been added and the rice is cooked. Be sure to stir continuously.
- Remove from the heat and add the cheese and tarragon. Add the mushrooms, salt, and pepper and serve.

nutritional analysis per serving
313.0 calories; 14.73 g fat (39% calories from fat); 11.23 g protein; 37.06 g carbohydrate; 15.18 mg cholesterol; 175.06 mg sodium

Prosciutto and Egg Pasta

PREP TIME: 30 minutes.
SERVE: Serves 4

My son prefers cured bacon in this recipe, but prosciutto works just as well, and it's what is used in this recipe in Italy. Mrs. Leepers rice noodles hold their shape well and are found in most health food stores or larger markets such as Wholefoods, Fresh Fields, and Wild Oats. You can also use a corn/quinoa pasta or spaghetti squash.

1 tablespoon olive oil

½ pound prosciutto, chopped

4 cloves garlic, chopped

¼ cup red wine

1 pound rice noodles

3 large eggs, beaten

¼ cup fresh parsley, or 1 tablespoons dried

1 cup Parmesan cheese

½ teaspoon freshly ground pepper

- Heat a large skillet to medium-high and cook the prosciutto until it is crispy, 3 to 5 minutes. Add the garlic and continue to cook until soft. Drain off any excess fat and add the wine. Reduce the heat to medium and cook, allowing the mixture to reduce. Turn off the heat.
- Meanwhile, cook the noodles according to the package directions. When you drain the noodles, immediately add the beaten eggs, and toss quickly to allow the eggs to cook quickly. Add the prosciutto mixture and parsley. Toss to mix well.
- Add the Parmesan cheese and toss well. Add pepper. Serve immediately.

> Note: When adding the raw eggs to this recipe, be sure to add them immediately after draining off the noodle water, so the noodles are very hot, and the eggs cook quickly. If they are runny, the noodles are not hot enough, and you will want to return the pan to the stove to heat through.

nutritional analysis per serving
426.52 calories; 17.46 g fat (37% calories from fat); 129.09 g protein; 31.09 g carbohydrate; 214.82 mg cholesterol; 1,800 mg sodium

Pumpkin Risotto

PREP TIME: 5 minutes to prepare and 30 minutes to cook
SERVE: Serves 6

This risotto is wonderful served with a salad, vegetable, and salmon. It also pares well with turkey, roast pork, or ham. Of course you don't have to serve it with meat or fish; it is great all by itself.

1 tablespoon olive oil

1 large red onion, chopped finely

1 teaspoon grated nutmeg

4 cups chicken or vegetable broth

½ cup white wine

1 (14-ounce) can pureed pumpkin

1 ½ cups arborio rice

½ cup Parmesan cheese, grated

2 cloves garlic, minced

Dash of freshly ground pepper

Dash of red pepper flakes

- In a large skillet or Dutch oven heat the olive oil over medium-high heat. Add the onion and sauté until soft, 4 to 5 minutes. Add the garlic and sauté 1 to 2 minutes longer. Add the arborio rice, and stir to lightly brown.
- Heat the chicken broth in a small saucepan until it boils. Keep it hot, and add one ladleful of broth to the rice mixture. Stir until the broth is absorbed, and then add another ladleful. Continue this process until all of the broth has been added and the rice is cooked through.
- Add the pumpkin and Parmesan cheese to the mixture and stir until well blended. Add the red pepper flakes and ground pepper. (I use a lot of ground pepper in this recipe.) Also add the nutmeg and stir until blended. Serve warm.

nutritional analysis per serving
183.40 calories; 5.50 g fat (28.60% calories from fat); 8.30 g protein; 22.60 g carbohydrate; 9 mg cholesterol; 900 mg sodium

Red Pepper and Butternut Risotto

PREP/COOK TIME: 1 hour
SERVE: Serves 6

This risotto is great any time of year, but winter is my favorite time to serve it. I created this recipe using up what I had in my refrigerator, so you can stray from the recipe to include your favorite vegetables, too. You can add up to ¾ cup of grated Swiss cheese in this recipe if you don't mind dairy, and fresh Parmesan, too.

1 pound butternut squash

4 tablespoons olive oil

1 large onion, chopped

2 cloves garlic, minced

2 red bell peppers, sliced finely

1 yellow bell pepper, sliced finely

1 cup arborio rice

5 cups vegetable broth

½ cup vegan Parmesan cheese

1 tablespoon tarragon, fresh if possible

Salt and pepper

- Steam or bake the butternut squash until soft. Peel and cube.
- Sauté the onion in the olive oil. Add the garlic and the peppers. Next, add the rice* and stir until it is well coated with oil.
- Heat the vegetable broth in a small pan and, once it is very hot, begin adding a ladleful at a time to the rice mixture. Stir until all the moisture is absorbed, then add another ladleful of stock. Continue adding the stock a little at a time. When all the stock has been added, or the rice is cooked, stir in the cheese and fresh tarragon. Remove from the heat and add the butternut squash. Season to taste.

Lentil arborio rice can be found at most health food stores and adds protein. It is a nice substitute for traditional arborio rice.

nutritional analysis per serving
307.05 calories; 10.42 g fat (28% calories from fat); 5.74 g protein; 50.59 g carbohydrate; 0 mg cholesterol; 182.56 mg sodium

Refried Beans

NO DAIRY, EGGS, OR NUTS

PREP/COOK TIME: 2 hours, not counting the soaking time
SERVE: Serves 8

This recipe is very basic. You can add chiles, peppers, or other vegetables to it, but I like to have a basic bean version around that I can use as a base for other dishes. This can be served along with rice or a salad, or used in tacos or burritos.

2 cups dried pinto beans

3 tablespoons olive oil

2 large onions, chopped

5 cloves garlic, chopped

2 teaspoons ground cumin

¼ teaspoon cayenne or freshly ground black pepper

1 teaspoon salt

- Soak the beans overnight. Drain the water and add fresh water. Cook for about 1½ hours, or until the beans are soft. Drain.
- Heat the oil in a large skillet and add the onion. Sauté over medium heat until the onion is soft, 5 to 8 minutes. Add the garlic and cumin, and continue cooking for another 3 to 4 minutes.
- Mash the beans in a large bowl and add to the onion mixture (mash with a fork or potato masher). Mix together well and heat through. Add the cayenne or freshly ground pepper and salt and serve.

nutritional analysis per serving
108.63 calories; 5.69 g fat (5.69% calories from fat); 3.30 g protein; 11.81 g carbohydrate; 0 mg cholesterol; 469.07 mg sodium

Spanish Rice

PREP TIME: 10 minutes to prepare and about 30 minutes to cook
SERVE: Serves 10

*With **big boys** to keep fed through the years, I found this recipe combined with burritos a quick, hearty meal. I love it by itself with guacamole on top and some salsa. Combined with a salad, you have a quick lunch or dinner that is not only good but easy to make.*

½ large red onion, chopped finely

½ large red bell pepper, chopped finely

¼ large green bell pepper, chopped finely

2 cloves garlic, chopped finely

1 large stalk celery, chopped finely

½ teaspoon ground cumin (can use less if desired)

¼ teaspoon dried oregano

¼ teaspoon freshly ground black pepper

¼ teaspoon sea salt

½ cup diced tomatoes

½ cup tomato sauce

1 cup chicken or vegetable broth

1 tablespoon olive oil

2 cups basmati white rice

3 cups water

- Place the chopped onion, bell peppers, garlic, and celery in a large mixing bowl. Add the herbs and spices, tomatoes, and tomato sauce. Mix, add the chicken broth and stir. Set aside.
- Heat a large skillet and heat the olive oil. Add the rice and heat until the rice begins to pop. Add the vegetables and water. Cook until most of the liquid has evaporated. When the rice begins to stick to the skillet, turn off the heat and cover. Let the skillet sit with the lid on for 5 minutes. Stir the rice, then replace the lid and steam-cook (with no heat) for another 15 minutes. Fluff and serve. Can be served with avocado and salsa

nutritional analysis per serving
161.60 calories; 1.60 g fat (9% calories from fat); 4.10 g protein; 32.10 g carbohydrate; 0 mg cholesterol; 272 mg sodium

Spicy Indian Vegetable Pilaf

PREP TIME: About 70 minutes
SERVE: Serves 8

Brown rice is *great, but adding vegetables and spices to it really makes it delightful. If you have a peanut allergy, substitute chopped cashews; it works just as well.*

3 tablespoons olive oil

1 large red onion, chopped finely

1 large red bell pepper, diced

4 cloves garlic, chopped finely

2 cups uncooked brown rice

¼ teaspoon ground cloves

½ teaspoon groundcumin

1 teaspoon ground cinnamon

1 teaspoon peeled and grated fresh ginger

4½ cups vegetable stock or water

1 cup green beans, cut into bite-size pieces

1 cup chopped carrots

1 cup chopped zucchini

¾ cup green peas (optional)

¾ cup peanuts, chopped (optional)

¼ teaspoon freshly ground pepper

Dash of salt, to taste

■ Heat the oil in a Dutch oven on medium heat. Sauté the onion and red bell pepper until soft, 4 to 5 minutes. Add the garlic, red bell pepper, rice, cloves, cumin, cinnamon, and ginger. Cook over medium heat for 2 to 3 minutes. Add the vegetable stock and stir well. Bring to a boil, add the green beans, carrots, and zucchini, and simmer for 45 to 55 minutes, or until the vegetables are tender and the rice is cooked. Add the peas and heat through, if using. If desired, top with chopped peanuts. Season to taste.

nutritional analysis per serving
395.0 calories; 15.0 g fat (33.3% calories from fat); 12.3 g protein; 55.20 g carbohydrate; 1.0 mg cholesterol; 867.0 mg sodium

salads and vegetables

Crab Louis

PREP TIME: 20 minutes
SERVE: Serves 2

Nothing beats fresh dungeness crab. *It's important to use fresh crab in this salad. Feel free to use another salad dressing if you prefer not to eat dairy, as there is sour cream in this dressing. You could use the tofu sour cream in place of dairy.*

⅓ pound cooked crab

2 green onions, minced

1 stalk celery, finely chopped

1 small red bell pepper, finely chopped

2 cups mixed greens, rinsed and drained

2 hard cooked eggs, shelled and sliced

1 firm avocado, peeled, pitted, and sliced thinly

Olives (optional)

Dressing:

¼ cup sour cream

3 tablespoons apple cider vinegar

3 tablespoons seafood sauce

1 tablespoon agave nectar or fruit sweetener

Salt and pepper, to taste

- In a large bowl, combine the crab and all vegetables except the greens and avocado. In a small bowl, mix together the dressing ingredients and add to the crab mixture. Toss to mix well. Cover and chill.

- Arrange the mixed greens on a plate and top with the salad ingredients. Place the sliced eggs and avocado on top, add the olives, if desired, and serve.

nutritional analysis per serving

473.78 calories; 29.75 g fat (54% of calories from fat); 26.07 g protein; 32.59 g carbohydrate; 280.82 mg cholesterol; 934.68 mg sodium

Apple-Pear Coleslaw

PREP TIME: 15 minutes to prepare and 2 hours to chill
SERVE: Serves 6

Walnuts work well in this salad, too. If you don't have any poppy seeds on hand, toss in a handful of nuts instead. This is a great snack salad for the kids after school, or for a school lunch.

½ head green cabbage, chopped finely

½ head red cabbage, chopped finely

½ cup radicchio, chopped finely

3 small carrots, grated

2 large apples, peeled, cored, and chopped

2 cups pears, peeled, cored, and chopped

⅛ cup canola oil

⅛ cup cider vinegar

1 tablespoon brown rice syrup

2 teaspoons poppy seeds

Dash of salt

¼ teaspoon freshly ground black pepper

- Place the green and red cabbage, radicchio, and carrots in a large bowl. Peel and chop the apples and pears. Add the apples and pears to the cabbage mixture.
- In a small bowl, combine the oil, vinegar, brown rice syrup, poppy seeds, salt, and pepper.
- Toss the dressing with the vegetables and fruit, and chill for at least 2 hours.

nutritional analysis per serving
118.17 calories; 4.80 g fat (36% calories from fat);
2.75 g protein; 19.31 g carbohydrate; 0 mg cholesterol;
219.31 mg sodium

Apple Quinoa Salad

NO DAIRY, EGGS, OR NUTS

PREP TIME: About 30 minutes
SERVE: Serves 4

If you struggle about what to eat for lunch, or what to send to school with the kids for lunch, try this salad. It is full of protein, complex carbohydrates, and tastes good. If the kids don't like raw onions, leave them out and add some celery instead. Feel free to experiment with this recipe. You can substitute mint for the parsley, replace the vegetable broth with apple juice, and use pears instead of apples. Be creative!

1 cup quinoa, well rinsed

2 cups water

½ small red bell pepper, chopped

⅓ cup red onion, chopped

½ cup carrot, grated

¼ cup parsley, fresh, chopped

¼ cup apple cider vinegar

2–3 tablespoons vegetable broth

Salt and pepper, to taste

¼ teaspoon ground cinnamon

1 clove garlic, minced

1 large organic apple, chopped

- Combine quinoa and water in a 2-quart saucepan. Bring to a boil over high heat. Once the water boils, reduce the heat to low and simmer for 10 to 15 minutes, or until light and fluffy. Set aside to cool.
- In a small bowl, combine the red bell pepper, red onion, grated carrot, parsley, cider vinegar, vegetable broth, salt, pepper, cinnamon, and garlic.
- Add to the cooled quinoa and stir to mix well. Add the chopped apples.

nutritional analysis per serving
134.30 calories; 1.80 g fat (11% calories from fat); 4.20 g protein; 26.47 g carbohydrate; 0 mg cholesterol; 21.39 mg sodium

Asian-Style Coleslaw

NO DAIRY, EGGS, OR NUTS

PREP TIME: 10 minutes
SERVE: Serves 4

The rice vinegar in this recipe provides that Asian feel. This is a good salad to take to a potluck, as everyone loves Chinese ramen salad, and this is a healthier version of that salad.

1 large carrot, peeled, and sliced thinly

1 cup red cabbage, sliced thinly

1½ cups green cabbage, sliced thinly

1 cup Napa cabbage, sliced thinly

3 ounces snow peas, sliced thinly

2 tablespoons chopped green onions

3 teaspoons rice wine vinegar

1 teaspoon dry mustard

½ teaspoon ground ginger

2 tablespoons vegetable oil

1 tablespoon Asian sesame oil

2 teaspoons wheat-free tamari sauce

Salt and pepper, to taste

- Combine the carrots and the red, green, and napa cabbage and place in a large bowl. Add the snow peas.
- In a small bowl, combine the rest of the ingredients, except the salt and pepper. Stir together well until the mustard and ginger dissolve and the oils and vinegar are well blended. Before serving, combine the dressing and slaw, and toss to coat. Season with salt and pepper if desired.

> This salad can be made ahead of time and stored in the refrigerator.

nutritional analysis per serving
119.52 calories; 8.42 g fat (62% of calories from fat); 2.45 g protein; 11.75 g carbohydrate; 0 mg cholesterol; 223.99 mg sodium

Black Bean, Red Pepper, Corn, and Quinoa Salad

PREP TIME: 15 minutes
SERVE: Serves 6

The quinoa adds a nutty flavor and protein to this salad. This recipe makes a lot, and the salad is very versatile. You can add other veggies to it, or toss in some chopped mango for a bite of sweetness.

½ cup quinoa, rinsed

1 cup vegetable broth or water

1 tablespoon olive oil

¼ teaspoon ground cumin

¼ teaspoon salt

¼ cup orange juice

½ teaspoon freshly ground pepper

1 (14-ounce) can black beans, drained

1 cup white corn (optional)

1 large tomato, chopped

1 large leek, chopped

3 tablespoons chopped cilantro

- Combine the quinoa with the vegetable broth in a saucepan. Bring to a boil and reduce the heat. Cook until light and fluffy, about 12 minutes. Cool.
- In a large bowl, mix the remaining ingredients together. Toss well. Add the quinoa and toss again to mix. Serve cold.

> This salad can be served over mixed greens. I often serve it as a dip.

nutritional analysis per serving

213.82 calories; 4.30 g fat (18% calories from fat); 8.96 g protein; 37.11 g carbohydrate; 0.41 mg cholesterol; 501 mg sodium

Black Bean and Rice Salad

PREP TIME: 10 to 15 minutes to prepare and 1 hour or longer to chill
SERVE: Serves 4

This salad is easy to make and provides a healthy dose of protein and complex carbohydrates. It can be stored in the refrigerator for several days and is a great meal for a quick lunch.

1 (15-ounce) can black beans, drained
3 cups cooked brown rice
¼ cup red onion, chopped finely
¼ cup chopped celery

Dressing:

1 teaspoon ground coriander
1 teaspoon ground cumin
3 tablespoons chopped cilantro
¼ cup orange juice
1 tablespoon balsamic vinegar
2 tablespoons olive oil
½ teaspoon ground cinnamon
Salt and pepper, to taste

- Mix the dressing ingredients together in a glass jar and shake to mix well.
- Combine the beans, rice, celery and onions in a bowl and add the dressing. Toss to mix well. Refrigerate to blend the flavors.

nutritional analysis per serving
356.63 calories; 8.98 g fat (22% calories from fat); 11.98 g protein; 58.66 g carbohydrate; 0 mg cholesterol; 215.88 mg sodium

Black Bean and Salsa Salad

NO DAIRY, EGGS, OR NUTS

PREP TIME: 10 minutes to prepare and 1 hour to chill
SERVE: Serves 6

This salad is great for a party. It's beautiful, keeps well in the fridge, and can even be served as an appetizer with vegetables on the side.

1 (15-ounce) can black beans, drained

⅓ cup frozen orange juice concentrate

2 jalapeño chile peppers, chopped

¼ cup lime juice

½ cup chopped cilantro

2 cups tomato, chopped

½ cup red onion, chopped

1 medium-size red bell pepper, chopped

1 medium-size green bell pepper, chopped

½ cup corn (optional)

1 large avocado, chopped

■ Mix all the ingredients together in a large bowl. Cover and place in the refrigerator for at least 1 hour. Stir well before serving.

nutritional analysis per serving
164.0 calories; 1.0 g fat (5.2% calories from fat); 9.10 g protein; 32.40 g carbohydrate; 0 mg cholesterol; 16.0 mg sodium

Fruity Chicken Salad

NO EGGS

PREP TIME: 15 to 20 minutes
SERVE: Serves 4

Feel free to use different fruits and berries in this recipe. This salad can be a meal in itself. It tastes good, looks wonderful, and keeps well for several days.

2 cups grilled, cubed chicken breasts

1 cup blueberries

1 cup raspberries

1 cup kiwi, peeled and cut into bite-size pieces

½ cup cantaloupe, peeled and cut into cubes

2 tablespoons feta cheese

3 tablespoons sliced or chopped almonds

1 head romaine hearts or organic mixed greens

Dressing:

2 tablespoons agave nectar

⅛ cup red wine vinegar

¼ cup olive oil

¼ cup fresh orange juice

¼ teaspoon freshly ground black pepper

Dash of salt

- In a large bowl, combine the cubed chicken breast, blueberries, raspberries, kiwi, cantaloupe, feta cheese, and almonds, and toss well to mix.
- In a separate bowl, combine the dressing ingredients. Toss over the salad ingredients. Serve this salad heaped on top of the lettuce leaves placed on serving dishes.

nutritional analysis per serving
294.69 calories; 7.62 g fat (23% calories from fat); 26.26 g protein; 35.03 g carbohydrate; 63.67 mg cholesterol; 149.77 mg sodium

Curried Chicken Salad with Greens

NO EGGS OR PEANUTS

PREP TIME: 20 minutes to prepare
SERVE: Serves 6

Tofu sour cream, which is made with soy, can replace the yogurt in this recipe. I have also used 4 ounces each of the dairy sour cream and cream cheese for a richer, smoother dressing. This salad is a crowd-pleaser.

1 stalk celery, sliced thinly

3 cups cooked and cubed chicken breast

8 ounces plain yogurt or plain soy yogurt

¼ cup mango chutney

2 teaspoon curry powder

1 cup seedless red grapes

½ cup almonds, sliced thinly

½ medium-size apple, peeled and chopped

½ cup feta cheese (optional)

Mixed salad greens

- Place all ingredients except the greens in a large mixing bowl. Toss to blend.
- Serve over mixed salad greens.

nutritional analysis per serving
436.0 calories; 12.39 g fat (25% of calories from fat); 41.85 g protein; 36.87 g carbohydrate; 90.22 mg cholesterol; 598.60 mg sodium

Greek Salad

NO EGGS OR NUTS

PREP TIME: 15 minutes
SERVE: Serves 4

We've all heard *the Mediterranean diet is good for us, and this is a typical Mediterranean salad. Enjoy it without guilt. It offers plenty of healthy fats, protein, and complex carbohydrates. To boost your protein, and omega-3s, add some canned sardines to the salad.*

1 small red onion, sliced thinly

1 medium-size cucumber, sliced thinly

10 kalamata olives, pitted

3 medium-size tomatoes, cut into wedges

1 medium green bell pepper, sliced thinly (optional)

½ cup feta cheese

Vinaigrette:

2 tablespoons olive oil

2 tablespoons red wine vinegar

½ teaspoon dried oregano

1 tablespoon chopped fresh flat-leaf parsley

¼ teaspoon salt

¼ teaspoon freshly ground pepper

1 clove garlic, minced

- In a large bowl, combine the onion, cucumber, kalamata olives, tomatoes, and bell pepper, if desired.
- In a small bowl, combine the vinaigrette ingredients, mixing well. Add the dressing to the salad ingredients and toss until well blended. Crumble the feta cheese over the salad and serve.
- You can also serve this salad over mixed greens.

nutritional analysis per serving
180.57 calories; 13.71 g fat (67% calories from fat); 4.34 g protein; 11.93 g carbohydrate; 16.69 mg cholesterol; 516.84 mg sodium

Jicama Fruit Salad

NO DAIRY, EGGS, OR NUTS

PREP TIME: 10 to 15 minutes
SERVE: Serves 6

Jicama is a root vegetable and doesn't get as much attention as it deserves. It adds a wonderful crunch to recipes, and its light flavor doesn't overpower the other ingredients. It's similar to tofu in that it takes on the flavors it is blended with.

1 large orange, peeled, sectioned, and sections cut in half

1 medium-size grapefruit, peeled, sectioned, and sections cut in half

½ pint strawberries, washed, hulled, and sliced

1 cup sliced cantaloupe

1 small jicama, peeled and sliced thinly

Dressing:

3 tablespoons orange juice

1 tablespoon agave nectar

1 teaspoon Dijon mustard

1 tablespoon sesame seeds

¼ cup canola oil

Dash of freshly ground black pepper

- Place the orange, grapefruit, strawberries, cantaloupe, and jicama in a large bowl.
- In a glass jar, mix together the orange juice and agave nectar. Shake to blend. Add the mustard and sesame seeds. Shake. Add the canola oil and pepper. Shake together until the mixture is well blended and slightly thick. Pour a small amount of dressing over the fruit mixture and toss well. Add more dressing as needed.

> This dressing works well as a marinade for chicken or other meats, too.

nutritional analysis per serving
181.03 calories; 10.83 g fat (52% calories from fat); 2.02 g protein; 21.74 g carbohydrate; 0 mg cholesterol; 19.43 mg sodium

Jimmy's Potato Salad

PREP TIME: 30 minutes
SERVE: Serves 10

This is an old family recipe. It was hard to get my father to provide exact amounts of herbs, so please feel free to adjust the seasonings to your preference. It is the best!

7–8 large hard-boiled eggs, peeled

7–8 large cooked potatoes, cooled and diced

1 (4-ounce) can black olives, sliced and drained

3 large dill pickles, chopped

4 stalks celery, chopped

½ cup green onions, chopped finely

1 cup mayonnaise

1 tablespoon dry mustard

2 tablespoons apple cider vinegar

3 teaspoons Johnny's Salad Elegance seasoning (or salt, paprika, and dried grated Parmesan cheese)

2 teaspoons dried parsley

Dash of paprika

Salt and pepper, to taste

- Chop six of the hard-boiled eggs and place in a large salad bowl. Add the potatoes, olives, dill pickles, celery, and green onions, and toss to mix well.
- Add the mayonnaise, mustard, vinegar, and Salad Elegance, and mix well with the potato mixture. Add salt and pepper to taste.
- Slice the remaining eggs and arrange on top of potato salad. Sprinkle with additional Salad Elegance, parsley, and paprika.

nutritional analysis per serving
296.26 calories; 13.46 g fat (40% calories from fat); 8.74 g protein; 37.14 g carbohydrate; 174.91 mg cholesterol; 908.12 mg sodium

Mango Salad

PREP TIME: 10 to 15 minutes
SERVE: Serves 4

What a great summertime salad. *Fresh fruit and herbs are a wonderful combination. Any berry will do in this salad, so mix it up. Try adding raspberries or blueberries, or use all three.*

- 1 large mango, peeled and cut into cubes
- 1 pint strawberries, washed and hulled
- 1 tablespoon canola oil
- 2 tablespoons orange juice or lime juice
- ¼ teaspoon ground cumin
- 2 tablespoons chopped fresh cilantro
- ¼ cup red bell pepper, diced
- 2 tablespoons red onion, sliced finely
- ¼ teaspoon red pepper flakes

- Mix all the ingredients together in a large bowl and toss to coat evenly. Season to taste with salt, if desired.

nutritional analysis per serving
108.65 calories; 1.91 g fat (15% calories from fat); 1.75 g protein; 24.14 g carbohydrate; 0 mg cholesterol; 4.61 mg sodium

Nutty Fruit Salad

NO DAIRY, EGGS, OR PEANUTS

PREP TIME: 1 hour
SERVE: Serves 4

Butter leaf lettuce can be expensive, so feel free to substitute organic romaine hearts. I often buy the organic hearts at either Trader Joe's or my local market.

4 large oranges

1 large. apple, peeled, cored, and chopped

1 large pear, peeled, cored, and cubed

½ cup orange juice, fresh if possible

2 tablespoons brown rice syrup or agave nectar

½ teaspoon ground cinnamon

3 tablespoons lime juice

3 tablespoons olive oil

½ cup currants

1 head butter leaf lettuce or romaine hearts

1 head Belgian endive

1 cup fresh mint leaves

½ cup spicy pecans or walnuts (see recipe page 50)

- Peel the oranges and remove the white pith. Separate into segments and place in a large bowl. Add the apple and pear to the oranges. Add the orange juice, the agave nectar, cinnamon, lime juice, and olive oil. Toss well with the fruit. Add the currants and toss.
- Wash the lettuce and endive, and toss together in a bowl with the mint leaves. When serving, top the lettuce mixture with the fruit and garnish with the nuts.

nutritional analysis per serving
445.08 calories; 21.32 g fat (41% calories from fat); 6.47 g protein; 67.74 g carbohydrate; 0 mg cholesterol; 50.03 mg sodium

Quinoa Tabbouleh Salad

PREP TIME: 20 to 25 minutes
SERVE: Serves 8

Traditional tabbouleh is made with couscous and that is a wheat grain, so this recipe replaces couscous with quinoa. I think you will be pleasantly surprised.

1 cup quinoa

1 cup vegetable broth

½ cup carrots, grated

1 stalk celery, chopped

1 cup diced tomatoes

1 cup diced cucumber

1 cup parsley, chopped

Dressing:

¼ cup lemon juice

⅛ cup olive oil

2 tablespoons minced garlic

2 tablespoons chopped fresh mint (or 2 teaspoons dried)

Salt and pepper, to taste

- Prepare the salad dressing by mixing together the lemon juice, oil, garlic, and mint.
- Rinse the quinoa well and place in a saucepan. Add the vegetable broth and bring to a boil. Reduce the heat and simmer over low heat for about 12 minutes, or until the broth is absorbed. Turn off the heat and let cool.
- Combine the carrots, celery, tomatoes, and cucumber in a large salad bowl and add the quinoa and parsley. Pour the dressing over the ingredients and toss well. Season with salt and pepper.

nutritional analysis per serving
196.10 calories; 6.97 g fat (31% calories from fat); 5.64 g protein; 29.26 g carbohydrate; 0.41 mg cholesterol; 488.71 mg sodium

Shrimp Salad

PREP TIME: 10 to 15 minutes
SERVE: Serves 4

This salad is very refreshing. You can jazz it up by adding in some sliced carrots, cucumbers, and tomatoes. This makes perfect leftovers for lunch. It stores well in the refrigerator for one to three days.

¾ pound medium-size shrimp, deveined and cooked

½ pound endive

½ pound butter leaf lettuce

2 firm avocados

1 small red bell pepper, chopped

¼ cup finely chopped green onions

3 tablespoons olive oil

2 teaspoons Dijon mustard

1 tablespoon fresh tarragon

2 tablespoons lemon juice

½ teaspoon black pepper

Salt, to taste

- Wash the endive and lettuce, and chop into 1-inch chunks.
- Slice the avocados. In a large bowl, mix together the pepper, onions, and avocados.
- Add the shrimp and lettuce, and toss well. Set aside.
- In a small bowl, combine the oil, mustard, tarragon, lemon juice, and pepper. Mix until the dressing is thick and smooth. Pour over the salad ingredients and toss until well mixed. Season with salt, if desired.

nutritional analysis per serving
404.47 calories; 29.83 g fat (63% calories from fat); 21.76 g protein; 17.37 g carbohydrate; 129.28 mg cholesterol; 765.70 mg sodium

Spinach and Pear Salad

PREP TIME: 30 minutes
SERVE: Serves 6

I love this salad, but you can mix it up by replacing the spinach with endive or mixed greens. I use fresh pears whenever possible but, when you can't get them, canned will do. Always choose organic whenever possible.

8 cups baby organic spinach, washed and torn into pieces

¾ cup Spicy Walnuts (see recipe page 51)

1 small red onion, chopped finely

1 small red bell pepper, chopped finely

12 ounces water-packed pears, chopped into bite-size pieces, or fresh pears (reserve liquid for dressing)

3 ounces Gorgonzola cheese, crumbled

Dressing:

2 teaspoons honey mustard or plain mustard

¼ cup juice from the canned pears

1 teaspoon balsamic vinegar

1 tablespoon olive oil

Salt and pepper, to taste

- Place the dressing ingredients into a glass jar and shake well to mix the ingredients together evenly. Season to taste, adding salt or pepper and mixing well.
- Place the spinach in a large salad bowl. Add the spicy walnuts, onion, pepper, and pears. Toss to mix well. Pour on the dressing and toss to mix well. Add the crumbled cheese on top, and serve.

nutritional analysis per serving
280.98 calories; 17.49 g fat (52.9% calories from fat); 11.51 g protein; 28.41 g carbohydrate; 19.16 mg cholesterol; 218.53 mg sodium

Sweet and Sour Broccoli Coleslaw

PREP TIME: 10 minutes to prepare and up to 2 hours to chill
SERVE: Serves 4

If you like crunch, this salad is for you. Between the broccoli and the jicama, you'll get a workout for your jaws. It is a quick, easy salad to make and you can add other vegetables if you have some you would like to use up. Toss in some chopped red bell pepper or some celery. You can also add cooked bacon bits, if you wish.

½ cup apple, peeled, cored, and shredded

3 cups broccoli, chopped finely

½ cup red onion, sliced thinly

½ cup almonds, sliced

½ cup raisins

½ cup jicama, peeled and sliced (optional)

Dressing:

¼ cup rice wine vinegar

1 tablespoon sesame oil

1 tablespoon agave nectar or fruit sweetener

⅛ teaspoon salt

- Mix together the dressing ingredients in a glass jar and shake well.
- Mix the salad ingredients together in a bowl and pour the dressing over all. Toss together and cover. Refrigerate for up to 2 hours. Toss again before serving.

nutritional analysis per serving

238.73 calories; 12.83 g fat (46% of calories from fat); 5.93 g protein; 36.36 g carbohydrate; 0 mg cholesterol; 91.40 mg sodium

Three-Bean Salad

PREP TIME: 30 minutes
SERVE: Serves 4

Bean salads are so good for you because they offer fiber and protein, and really fill you up. This salad is no exception. Experiment by using other beans, such as wax beans, soybeans, and black beans. Feel free to serve this as is, or on top of a bed of lettuce.

2 cups fresh green beans

1 cup cooked chickpeas (canned are okay)

1 cup cooked kidney beans (canned are okay)

¼ cup thinly sliced red onion

¼ cup minced red bell pepper

1 large tomato, diced

2 tablespoons olive oil

2 tablespoons Dijon mustard

2 tablespoons vinegar

1 tablespoon chopped fresh basil, or 1½ teaspoons dried

1 teaspoon fruit sweetener or agave nectar

¼ teaspoon freshly ground black pepper (or to taste)

Salt, to taste

- Steam the green beans about 5 minutes, or until crisp-tender. Cool. Place in a large bowl. Add the chickpeas, kidney beans, onion, pepper, and tomato. Mix together.
- In a glass jar, combine the oil, mustard, vinegar, basil, fruit sweetener, and pepper. Shake vigorously. Pour over the salad. Toss well. Let stand 20 minutes before serving.

nutritional analysis per serving
163.50 calories; 1.49 g fat (8% calories from fat); 8.22 g protein; 31.54 g carbohydrate; 0 mg cholesterol; 496.0 mg sodium

Carrots with Ginger

NO DAIRY, EGGS, OR NUTS

PREP/COOK TIME: 20 to 25 minutes
SERVE: Serves 6

Steamed carrots are good, but these are better! The orange and ginger really provide a wonderful flavor. You can also use real butter if you aren't avoiding dairy products.

1 pound carrots

2 tablespoons buttery vegan spread

1 tablespoons agave nectar

½ cup unsweetened orange juice

¼ teaspoon peeled and grated fresh ginger

½ teaspoon salt

¼ teaspoon freshly ground black pepper

■ Wash the carrots well and slice into ¼-inch disks. Steam the carrots in a steamer or in a saucepan with a small amount of water for about 15 minutes, or until tender. Once the carrots are cooked, place the shortening in a skillet and stir in the agave nectar. Add the orange juice and carrots and simmer for 5 minutes. Add the ginger, salt, and pepper and cook until it is heated through and a nice glaze develops.

nutritional analysis per serving
110.25 calories; 3.90 g fat (32% calories from fat);
1.28 g protein; 18.85 g carbohydrate; 0 mg cholesterol;
286.71 mg sodium

Cauliflower Curry

PREP/COOK TIME: 40 minutes
SERVE: Serves 4

This recipe will make you like cauliflower if you don't already. The curry in
this recipe is not overpowering, and if
you want to try something different,
use coconut milk in place of the
yogurt. It will also make the recipe
dairy free.

3 teaspoons olive oil

1 tablespoon peeled and finely
   chopped fresh ginger

1 large onion, chopped

1 cup chopped tomatoes

1 large yellow bell pepper, sliced

2 tablespoons curry powder (see
   box)

1 large head cauliflower, washed
   and chopped coarsely

3 cloves garlic, minced

1 cup nonfat yogurt

1 tablespoon lemon juice

1 teaspoon salt

½ teaspoon freshly ground
   pepper

■ Place the oil in a skillet or Dutch oven. Add
the ginger, onion, tomato, and bell pepper,
and sauté over medium heat for 4 minutes.
Reduce the heat and add the curry powder,
cauliflower, and garlic, stirring well to coat
the veggies. Cook for 1 minute. Add the
yogurt and bring to a boil. Turn the heat to
low and cover. Cook for 25 minutes, or until
the cauliflower is cooked through. Add the
lemon juice, salt, and pepper.

nutritional analysis per serving
102.94 calories; 3.82 g fat (33% calories from fat);
4.81 g protein; 13.93 g carbohydrate; 1.25 mg cholesterol; 351.56 mg sodium

---

Curry Powder:

In a small bowl combine the following:

½ teaspoon ground cardamom

½ teaspoon ground cinnamon

½ teaspoon ground coriander

¼ teaspoon ground cloves

½ teaspoon ground cumin

¼ teaspoon ground turmeric

¼ teaspoon chile powder

Delicious Pan-Style Potatoes

NO DAIRY OR NUTS

PREP/COOK TIME: 30 minutes to prepare
SERVE: Serves 4

These potatoes are very good as they are, but you can make a breakfast dish by omitting the Worcestershire sauce and adding 1 cup of chopped zucchini and mushrooms to the skillet with the oil and potatoes. Season with the salt and pepper and perhaps a pinch of fresh rosemary.

- 4 medium-size red potatoes, cut into ½-inch cubes
- 3 teaspoons oil
- ½ teaspoon salt
- ¼ teaspoon black pepper
- ½ cup chopped green onions
- 2 tablespoons chopped fresh parsley
- 1 tablespoon Worcestershire sauce
- 1 tablespoon chopped garlic

■ Cook the potatoes in boiling water for 4 to 5 minutes until almost tender. Drain and cool slightly. Heat the oil in a large skillet over medium heat. Add the potatoes. Cook, stirring often, for 12 to 15 minutes until the potatoes are golden brown and crisp. Add the green onions, parsley, Worcestershire sauce, and garlic. Cook until well blended, about 1 minute. Season with salt and pepper. Serve hot.

nutritional analysis per serving
219.25 calories; 10.31 g fat (42% of calories from fat); 3.59 g protein; 29.51 g carbohydrate; 0 mg cholesterol; 339.24 mg sodium

Fried Plantains

PREP/COOK TIME: 10 minutes
SERVE: Serves 4

I have spent quite a bit of time in Florida, and fried plantains are a Cuban dish commonly found there. I loved them, and came home to create my own version. This recipe is very basic, but you can spice it up by adding a dash of cayenne pepper and a teaspoon of grated fresh ginger.

2 large plantains, ripe
2 tablespoons olive oil
¼ teaspoon salt
Dash of freshly ground pepper

■ Peel the plantains and slice lengthwise. In a large skillet, heat the olive oil over medium-high heat. Add the plantains, and cook 3 to 4 minutes on each side. They should be lightly browned and soft. Sprinkle with salt and pepper, and serve.

nutritional analysis per serving
149.95 calories; 7.02 g fat (41% calories from fat); 0.96 g protein; 23.60 g carbohydrate; 0 mg cholesterol; 148.51 mg sodium

Garlic Mashed Potatoes

PREP/COOK TIME: 40 minutes to prepare
SERVE: Serves 6

The garlic in this recipe adds such a great flavor to these potatoes. You can substitute yams for potatoes if you'd like—yams are rated 25 on the glycemic index and white potatoes are rated 52.

2½ pounds potatoes, washed and peeled

1 head garlic

7 tablespoons buttery spread, melted

2 tablespoons white rice flour

1 cup soy milk, heated to a boil

Parsley

Salt and pepper, to taste

- Preheat the oven to 325°F.
- Melt 5 tablespoons of the shortening.
- Break up the head of garlic and place all of the cloves, with their skins on, on a baking dish. Drizzle with the melted buttery spread and roast in the oven for about 30 minutes, or until soft. Remove from the oven and remove the skins. Mash the garlic with the remaining 2 tablespoons of buttery spread in a skillet over medium heat. Add the flour and stir to thicken. Slowly add the soy milk a little bit at a time, stirring constantly, until the mixture is smooth and thick.
- Meanwhile, boil the potatoes until done, about 15 minutes. Mash them and add the garlic mixture. Stir to mix well. Add additional soy milk if needed, and stir in the parsley, salt and pepper. Serve hot.

> You can substitute butter for buttery spread if you prefer—but then it won't be dairy free.

nutritional analysis per serving
336.62 calories; 14.20 g fat (39% of calories from fat); 5.49 g protein; 46.40 g carbohydrate; 0 mg cholesterol; 158.35 mg sodium

Grilled Portobello Mushrooms

PREP/COOK TIME: 15 minutes
SERVE: Serves 2

This is a quick, easy recipe that will provide enough food for two. If you wish to serve more, double the recipe. These mushrooms store well in the refrigerator and taste great as leftovers.

2 large portobello mushrooms
Olive oil or vegetable oil spray
Salt
Pepper
2 teaspoons olive oil
1 cup finely chopped onions
3 cloves garlic
2 cups spinach, chopped
¼ cup chopped walnuts
½ teaspoon freshly ground pepper
½ teaspoon dried marjoram
½ teaspoon dried rosemary
2 tablespoons white wine

- Heat the grill or broiler.
- To prepare the mushrooms, remove the stems and baste with olive oil or spray with vegetable oil. Sprinkle the mushrooms with salt and pepper, and grill on each side until tender, about 4 minutes. If using a broiler, keep a careful eye on the mushrooms so they do not burn. Set aside.
- In a large skillet heat the olive oil over medium heat. Add the onions, garlic, spinach, and walnuts and saute for 4 to 5 minutes, or until soft. Add the herbs and wine, and continue cooking until the liquid is absorbed. Place the mushrooms cap side down on a serving dish and fill with the vegetable mixture. Season with more salt and pepper, if desired.

nutritional analysis per serving
246.43 calories; 14.67 g fat (51% calories from fat); 9.20 g protein; 23.35 g carbohydrate; 0 mg cholesterol; 40.36 mg sodium

New Potatoes and Herbs

NO DAIRY, EGGS, OR NUTS

PREP TIME: 10 minutes to prepare and 20 minutes to cook
SERVE: Serves 8

Roasted new potatoes are a perfect side dish to just about anything. I love them served with salmon, but they are great with any meat or fish. Use fresh herbs if possible.

3 pounds new potatoes
2 tablespoons olive oil
1 small sweet onion
1 tablespoon minced garlic
1 tablespoon dried basil
1 tablespoon dried oregano
1 tablespoon dried parsley
1 tablespoon dried rosemary
Salt and pepper, to taste

■ Wash the potatoes and then steam until tender. Set aside. Heat the olive oil in a large skillet and sauté the onion until soft, about 4 minutes. Add the garlic and continue to cook for 1 minute. Add the potatoes and herbs, and toss well. Sauté for about 10 minutes, or until the potatoes are heated through. Season to taste with salt and pepper, if desired.

nutritional analysis per serving
61.82 calories; 3.73 g fat (20% calories from fat);
3.55 g protein; 29.14 g carbohydrate; 0 mg cholesterol;
12.10 mg sodium

Quinoa Stuffing

NO DAIRY, EGGS, OR PEANUTS

PREP/COOK TIME: 30 minutes
SERVE: Serves 10

The ladies taking my cooking class all raved about this dish. I stuffed Cornish game hens with this stuffing, and then had enough left over to prepare a separate casserole. Once you make this, you'll want to make it again and again. You don't have to use it as a stuffing; I often serve it as a side dish. It's beautiful to look at and tastes divine.

4 tablespoons olive oil

1 medium-size red onion, minced

1 small butternut squash, peeled, seeded, and diced

1 small red bell pepper, chopped

2 cloves garlic, minced

1 large apple, peeled, cored, and chopped

1 cup mushrooms, sliced

1 tablespoon dried sage

Salt and freshly ground pepper

4 cups water

3 bay leaves

2 cups quinoa

1 cup dried cranberries

½ cup chopped fresh parsley

½ cup chopped pecans

Juice of 1 lime

■ Heat 3 tablespoons of the oil in a large skillet. Sauté the onion, squash, pepper, garlic, apples, and mushrooms over medium heat until the onion is soft and the squash is browned. Add the sage, salt, and pepper to taste. Set aside.

■ Bring 4 cups of water to a boil. Add the bay leaves and quinoa. After the water comes to a boil again, reduce the heat to low and cover. Cook for about 20 minutes. Remove from the heat and discard the bay leaves. Combine the sautéed vegetables and quinoa. Add the remaining oil. Add the dried cranberries, fresh parsley, lime juice, and pecans. Toss and serve.

nutritional analysis per serving
427.94 calories; 8.84 g fat (16% calories from fat); 6.08 g protein; 83.81 g carbohydrate; 0 mg cholesterol; 72.27 mg sodium

Roasted Green Beans

PREP/COOK TIME: 15 to 20 minutes
SERVE: Serves 4

Fresh green beans in the summer are wonderful in this recipe. I can't make enough it seems, they are so popular. If you don't have herbes de Provence, use a pinch of rosemary, thyme, oregano, and marjoram.

1 pound green beans, trimmed
2 teaspoons extra-virgin olive oil
¼ teaspoon freshly ground pepper
1 teaspoon herbes de Provence
1 tablespoon balsamic vinegar

- Heat the oven to 450°F. Place all of the ingredients except the balsamic vinegar in a shallow baking pan and stir until blended well.
- Bake for about 12 minutes, or until the beans are tender. Stir once during cooking. Remove from the oven and splash balsamic vinegar on the beans just prior to serving.

nutritional analysis per serving
88.19 calories; 2.79 g fat (28% calories from fat);
3.61 g protein; 12.99 g carbohydrate; 0 mg cholesterol;
5.88 mg sodium

Roasted Squash with Herbs

NO DAIRY, EGGS, OR NUTS

PREP TIME: 10 minutes to prepare and 30 minutes to bake
SERVE: Serves 4

You can use any kind of squash in this recipe. This dish is wonderful served with pork, chicken, or fish.

2 tablespoons olive oil

6 cups butternut squash, peeled, seeded, and cubed

2 cloves garlic, chopped

2 large onions, quartered

1 large red bell pepper, chopped

½ pound mushrooms, sliced

½ teaspoon salt

½ teaspoon pepper

2 teaspoons herbes de Provence

- Preheat the oven to 425°F.
- Lightly coat a 9 × 11-inch baking dish with 1 tablespoon of the olive oil. Place the squash cubes in the bottom of the dish. Add the garlic, onions, peppers, mushrooms, salt, pepper, and herbes de Provence. Bake for 30 minutes, or until browned and tender. Whenever you roast vegetables, it is important to turn or stir them occasionally. Be sure to do this halfway through the cooking time.

nutritional analysis per serving
189.06 calories; 7.25 g fat (34% calories from fat); 4.49 g protein; 31.71 g carbohydrate; 0 mg cholesterol; 303.35 mg sodium

Roasted Vegetables

PREP TIME: 10 minutes to prepare and 1 hours to roast/bake

SERVE: Serves 6

This recipe is a definite crowd-pleaser. I have taken it to many a Thanksgiving dinner and potluck and it's very popular. I love the vegetable combination given here, but I have friends who have called to tell me how good it is with other vegetables, too. So try this, and then in the summer when you have an abundance of vegetables at your disposal, try adding others to the mix.

1 large sweet potato

1 large yam

2 large onions

½ pound mushrooms

1 large red bell pepper

4 large carrots

4 cloves garlic, peeled

Olive oil

2 teaspoons fresh or dried oregano

2 teaspoons chopped fresh parsley

¼ cup fresh chopped basil

½ teaspoon pepper

¼ teaspoon salt

- Preheat the oven to 325°F.
- Wash all the vegetables and cut or quarter them into pieces of equal size. Leave the cloves of garlic whole.
- Drizzle a small amount of olive oil in the bottom of a 9 × 11-inch baking dish, and layer the veggies on the bottom. Sprinkle the herbs, salt, and pepper on top of the veggies, and drizzle a little more olive oil on top.
- Bake for up to 1 hour, or until tender. About halfway through the cooking time, stir the veggies so they do not dry out, making sure they are covered with oil. Keep an eye on them; you want them to be soft and crunchy, not dry. Cooking time may vary.

nutritional analysis per serving
174.81 calories; 7.38 g fat (37% calories from fat);
3.67 g protein; 26.30 g carbohydrate; 0 mg cholesterol;
165.08 mg sodium

Sautéed Green Beans

PREP TIME: 15 minutes
SERVE: Serves 4

This vegetable dish *is quick and easy to make and is a good side dish for the Basil Chicken Curry on page 83 or the Shrimp Curry on page 119. It has an Asian flavor.*

2 pounds fresh green beans, washed and trimmed

1 tablespoon sesame oil

2 tablespoons vegetable stock

½ pound mushrooms, sliced thinly

2 cloves garlic

2 teaspoons peeled and grated fresh ginger

1 teaspoon wheat-free tamari sauce

■ Steam the beans for about 8 minutes, or until crisp-tender. In a wok or large skillet, heat the oil and vegetable stock. Add the beans, mushrooms, garlic, and fresh ginger. Sauté for 2 to 3 minutes or until the mixture is heated through. Add the tamari sauce and continue to cook until the mixture thickens and the vegetables are tender.

nutritional analysis per serving
125.86 calories; 3.92 g fat (27% calories from fat); 6.39 g protein; 20.94 g carbohydrate; 0 mg cholesterol; 104.69 mg sodium

Sautéed Spinach

NO DAIRY, EGGS, OR NUTS

PREP TIME: 15 minutes to prepare and about 10 minutes to cook
SERVE: Serves 4

This green vegetable is good for you, and takes only a few minutes to make. It's best made with fresh spinach, but you can use frozen. If you use frozen though, be sure to drain out the excess water before sautéing.

4 cups fresh spinach, chopped (or 10 ounces frozen)

2 tablespoons olive oil

1 large red onion, chopped

3 cloves garlic, chopped

½ pound mushrooms, chopped

2 teaspoons balsamic vinegar

■ Wash the spinach thoroughly and steam until wilted, about 5 minutes.

■ In a small skillet, sauté the onion, garlic, and mushrooms. Add the spinach to the mixture and then splash with the balsamic vinegar.

nutritional analysis per serving
103.62 calories; 7.22 g fat (61% calories from fat); 3.26 g protein; 8.63 g carbohydrate; 0 mg cholesterol; 27.43 mg sodium

Scalloped Potatoes

NO EGGS OR NUTS

PREP TIME: 10 minutes to prepare and 60 minutes to bake
SERVE: Serves 8

Just like grandma used to make, only
I've left out the ham. If you want to add
more protein, add chopped cooked
ham or cooked prosciutto. It takes a
while to bake, but it's worth the wait.
Coat the baking dish with a vegetable
oil spray to avoid sticking.

2 tablespoons olive oil

1½–2 tablespoons arrowroot

2¼ cups soy milk

½ teaspoon fresh or dried thyme

½ teaspoon fresh rosemary

¾ cup Gorgonzola cheese

½ teaspoon sea salt

¼ teaspoon freshly ground
   pepper

3 pounds potatoes, washed,
   peeled, and sliced thin

½ large onion, chopped finely

4 cloves roasted garlic, sliced

Parmesan cheese, if desired

- Preheat the oven to 375°F.
- In a saucepan, heat the olive oil over medium-high heat and add the arrowroot. Whisk together and cook for 1 minute. Slowly add the soy milk, stirring constantly to keep the mixture from sticking to the pan. Add more soy milk if needed. When the mixture has thickened, add the herbs and cheese.
- Cook for 1 to 2 minutes, or until the cheese has melted. Remove from heat and add the salt and pepper.
- Cover a 9 × 13-inch glass baking dish with a layer of the sliced potatoes. Add a layer of onion and roasted garlic. Pour some of the cheese mixture on top, and add another layer of potatoes. Continue until you end with the last of the cheese mixture. Sprinkle some parmesan cheese on top, if desired, and bake for 30 minutes, covered. Uncover the baking dish and cook for another 30 minutes, or until the potatoes are tender when tested with a fork.
- You can also add cooked ham or Canadian bacon to this recipe.

nutritional analysis per serving
208.56 calories; 5.54 g fat (23% calories from fat); 6.49 g protein; 34.76 g carbohydrate; 2.37 mg cholesterol; 229.78 mg sodium

Stuffed Squash with Yam Puree

PREP/COOK TIME: 2 hours including baking time
SERVES: 8 to 10 (½ acorn squash per person)

This puree is great by itself, served during the holidays when everyone else is preparing their yams with marshmallows and tons of brown sugar! I have made this using butternut squash and it was very good. Cut the squash in half, as you would the acorn kind, scoop out the seeds, and then roast.

Yam Puree:

3 pounds yams (about 6–7 average-size red yams)

2–3 tablespoons butter or dairy-free shortening

⅓ cup agave cactus nectar or honey

¼ teaspoon sea salt

½–¾ teaspoon ground cinnamon

⅛ teaspoon grated nutmeg, fresh if possible

2 teaspoons crystallized ginger, or fresh, peeled and finely chopped

1 teaspoon orange peel

Squash:

4–5 acorn squashes

¼ cup agave cactus nectar

Zest of 2 oranges

1 teaspoon ground ginger

2 tablespoons butter or dairy-free shortening, melted

Fresh sage leaves

- To make the puree, bake or boil the yams (if you bake them, wash and poke with fork in several places. Place directly on oven rack and bake in a preheated 350°F oven until soft, about 1 hour.
- Once the yams have cooled, peel them and place them in a food processor or large bowl. If using a food processor, beat until smooth. If using an electric mixer, mix on low until the mixture becomes easy to work with. Increase speed and continue to mix until smooth. Add the agave nectar, herbs, butter, ginger, orange peel, and salt. Continue to mix until well blended.

To prepare the squash, do the following:
- Preheat the oven to 400°F.
- Cut each squash in half and scoop out the seeds and pulp. Place on a baking sheet. In a small bowl, mix together the butter, agave nectar, orange zest, and ground ginger. Drizzle this mixture over each squash half, and then place one sage leaf on each half. Bake for 30 to 40 minutes, or until soft. Remove from the oven and discard the sage leaves. Put a scoopful of the yam puree in each squash half and bake at 400°F until heated through, about 20 minutes.

nutritional analysis per serving
310.74 calories; 6.12 g fat (17% calories from fat); 3.48 g protein; 63.69 g carbohydrate; 15.05 mg cholesterol; 56.37 mg sodium

Sweet Potato Fries

PREP/COOK TIME: 30 minutes

SERVE: Serves 4

Oh boy—French fries that you don't have to feel guilty about. I love these! So do my kids. They are baked, not fried, and they are yams, not white potatoes. Need I say more?

4 small yams

Olive oil or vegetable oil spray

¼ teaspoon salt

⅛ teaspoon freshly ground pepper

⅛ teaspoon grated nutmeg

1 tablespoon olive oil

- Preheat the oven to 450°F.
- Scrub the yams and cut into quarters, then again into wedges. Place in a single layer on a cookie sheet that has been sprayed with a vegetable cooking spray or olive oil. Combine the salt, pepper, nutmeg, and olive oil. Brush on the potatoes and bake for about 20 minutes, or until they are browned and crunchy.

nutritional analysis per serving
208.97 calories; 3.82 g fat (16% calories from fat); 2.31 g protein; 41.90 g carbohydrate; 0 mg cholesterol; 158.98 mg sodium

Veggies with Herbes de Provence

PREP TIME: 10 minutes to prepare and 40 to 50 minutes to bake
SERVE: Serves 4

I happen to love butternut squash, but there are many other squashes to choose from, and they will all work well in this recipe. Toss in some carrots for color and a really beautiful dish.

2 tablespoons olive oil

½ pound mushrooms, cut in half

2–4 cloves garlic, cut in half

1 large red bell pepper, sliced

6 cups butternut squash, seeded, peeled, and cut into cubes

2 large onions, quartered

2 teaspoons herbes de Provence

½ teaspoon salt

½ teaspoon freshly ground pepper

- Preheat the oven to 400°F.
- Prepare an 11 × 13-inch baking dish by lightly coating it with 1 tablespoon of the oil. Place the mushrooms, garlic, peppers, squash, and onions in the dish, and drizzle with the rest of the olive oil. Sprinkle with the herbes de Provence, salt, and pepper. Bake for 40 to 50 minutes or until the vegetables are tender and browned. Be sure to stir the vegetables occasionally.

nutritional analysis per serving
189.06 calories; 7.25 g fat (34% of calories from fat); 4.49 g protein; 31.71 g carbohydrate; 0 mg cholesterol; 303.35 mg sodium

sauces

Barbecue Sauce

NO DAIRY, EGGS, OR NUTS

PREP TIME: 5–10 minutes
SERVE: Serves 4

I use this sauce for the Barbequed Spareribs found on page 82. To use for chicken, cut the water to ½ cup so it will be thicker and then baste the chicken before putting in the oven, and baste again two to three times while it roasts.

¾ cup ketchup

1 teaspoon salt

½ teaspoon Dijon mustard

1 cup water

1 tablespoon brown rice syrup

¼ teaspoon Tabasco

¼ teaspoon chile powder

■ Mix all the ingredients together in a large bowl. Use immediately or refrigerate for use later. This sauce is great on spareribs. It can also be used for chicken. I usually double the recipe and add sliced onions.

nutritional analysis per serving
42.76 calories; 0.15 g fat (3% calories from fat);
0.57 g protein; 11.46 g carbohydrate; 0 mg cholesterol;
768.33 mg sodium

Basil-Tomato Vinaigrette

PREP TIME: 5 to 6 minutes ■ **SERVE:** Serves 18

Here's a tip about basil: I buy it in the summer at the farmers' market, or grow it myself and then freeze it in zip-top bags for future use. Any time a recipe calls for fresh basil, I simply pull the bag from the freezer, and crush the frozen herb into the measuring cup. It works wonderfully.

8–10 fresh basil leaves

6 tablespoons olive oil

4 tablespoons white balsamic vinegar

1 clove garlic, minced

2 large tomatoes, crushed

½ teaspoon salt

■ Place all the ingredients in a blender and process for 1 minute, or until the mixture is well blended. Keep in the refrigerator.

nutritional analysis per serving
42.57 calories; 4.53 g fat (94% calories from fat); 0.12 g protein; 0.73 g carbohydrate; 0 mg cholesterol; 65.28 mg sodium

Berry Sauce

PREP TIME: 15 minutes ■ **SERVE:** Serves 16

This sauce is wonderful over the crêpes/blintzes. It's also great served over the almond torte and over the brown rice pudding. Go for it!

3½ cups frozen blueberries

1 cup frozen strawberries

⅓ cup fruit sweetener or agave nectar

½ cup water

2 tablespoons arrowroot

1 teaspoon ground cinnamon, if desired

■ Place the berries and fruit sweetener in a heavy saucepan. Bring to boil.

■ Mix together the water and arrowroot in a bowl and slowly whisk it into the berry mixture as it boils. Stir constantly. After the mixture comes to a boil again, turn the heat down to low and simmer for 5 to 7 minutes. Remove from the heat, sprinkle with cinnamon, and serve warm or refrigerate. Keeps up to 3 weeks in the refrigerator.

nutritional analysis per serving
40.19 calories; 0.14 g fat (3% calories from fat); 0.31 g protein; 11.27 g carbohydrate; 0 mg cholesterol; 0.62 mg sodium

Caper Sauce

NO EGGS OR NUTS

PREP TIME: 15 minutes ■ **SERVE:** Serves 6

This recipe came from my father, who serves this sauce over leg of lamb (page 114). It's also a great sauce for Roast Pork Tenderloins (page 115), and works over the potato scones on page 37. Prepare with margarine and soy milk for a dairy0free version.

¼ cup butter or buttery spread

1 tablespoon brown rice flour or arrowroot

1 cup soy milk or milk

3 tablespoons capers

Dash of salt

¼ teaspoon freshly ground black pepper

■ Melt the butter in a saucepan and add the flour. Cook until thick. Slowly add the milk, stirring constantly. Simmer on low for several minutes, adding more milk if it becomes too thick. Add the capers and heat through. Season with salt and pepper.

nutritional analysis per serving
111.24 calories; 8.39 g fat (68% calories from fat); 1.64 g protein; 7.33 g carbohydrate; 0 mg cholesterol; 213.25 mg sodium

Falafel Sauce

NO DAIRY, EGGS, OR NUTS

PREP TIME: 10 minutes ■ **SERVE:** Serves 8, ¼ cup per serving

Tradionally falafel sauce is made with yogurt. I left it out, but you can certainly add it back: reduce the amount of water, or replace it altogether with plain yogurt.

Feel free to add some grated cucumbers, too; they are very refreshing.

½ cup water

1 cup sesame tahini

3 cloves garlic, minced

½ cup lemon juice

1 tablespoon chopped parsley

Dash of freshly ground pepper

■ Place all of the ingredients in a blender or food processor, and process until smooth. Serve over falafels.

nutritional analysis per serving
183.15 calories; 15.91 g fat (73% calories from fat); 5.35 g protein; 8.14 g carbohydrate; 0 mg cholesterol; 47.48 mg sodium

O'Brien Family Spaghetti Sauce

PREP TIME: 20 minutes to prepare and 1 to 2 hours to cook
SERVE: Serves 12

This is an old family favorite. My father adds pork sausage to his version, *but I prefer this healthier version. I like to simmer this for at least 2 hours, if not longer, on the lowest setting possible. The flavors really meld together after a few hours. Serve over spaghetti squash or your favorite rice noodles.*

1 pound ground turkey or extra-lean beef

2 tablespoons olive oil

1 large onion, chopped

2 stalks celery, chopped

2 celery tops, chopped

3 cloves garlic, minced

1 (14-ounce) can tomato sauce

1 (6-ounce) can tomato paste

1 pound whole tomatoes, chopped

1 tablespoon basil, fresh if possible

2 teaspoons dried oregano

3 bay leaves

1 tablespoon dried parsley

1 cup chicken stock

½ cup white or red wine

Salt and pepper

Parmesan cheese, if desired

- Sauté the meat in a skillet over medium-high heat until cooked through. Drain and set aside.
- Chop all the veggies and sauté in the olive oil in a large skillet over a medium heat for 3 to 4 minutes. Add meat, tomato sauce, tomato paste, whole tomatoes, herbs, and chicken stock. Reduce the heat and simmer for 1 to 2 hours. Add the wine and continue simmering until the sauce is thick and flavorful. Season with salt and pepper, and serve over noodles. Top with Parmesan cheese if desired.

> I like to simmer this sauce all day to blend the flavors fully.

nutritional analysis per serving
137.80 calories; 9.90 g fat (57.7% calories from fat); 8.30 g protein; 6.60 g carbohydrate; 26.0 mg cholesterol; 642.2 mg sodium

Peach Salsa

PREP TIME: 10 minutes to prepare and 1 hour to chill
SERVE: Serves 6

This salsa works well with chicken, pork, salmon, and halibut. I like it served over barbequed chicken with a side of sweet potato fries.

2 large peaches, chopped

½ small red onion, chopped finely

½ cup red bell pepper, chopped

1 large avocado, peeled, pitted, and chopped

1 teaspoon peeled and grated fresh ginger (more to taste)

2 tablespoons cilantro, chopped

2 tablespoons olive oil

3 tablespoons lime juice

1 tablespoon brown rice syrup

¼ teaspoon freshly ground pepper

- In a medium-size bowl combine the peach, onion, bell pepper, avocado, ginger, and cilantro.
- In a small bowl whisk together the oil, lime juice, brown rice syrup, and ground pepper. Pour over the peach mixture and toss to coat. Refrigerate for 1 hour before serving. Season with salt, if desired.

nutritional analysis per serving
172.51 calories; 10.60 g fat (52% calories from fat);
1.36 g protein; 20.40 g carbohydrate; 0 mg cholesterol;
11.54 mg sodium

Spicy Peanut Sauce

NO DAIRY OR EGGS

PREP TIME: 10 minutes
SERVE: Serves 6

I love peanut sauce served over rice noodles, but it also tastes great served with grilled prawns, veggie kabobs, or chicken sauté. If you prefer a stronger peanut flavor, cut back on the sesame butter and increase the peanut butter.

¼ cup sesame or almond butter

¼ cup peanut butter

⅛ teaspoon tamari sauce

3 tablespoons lime juice

1 teaspoon brown rice syrup

3 tablespoons light coconut milk

1 teaspoon peeled and finely minced fresh ginger

1 clove garlic, minced

Black pepper, to taste

■ Put the sesame butter and peanut butter in a bowl and mix together. Add the tamari sauce, lime juice, brown rice syrup, and coconut milk, and stir to blend together. Add the ginger, garlic, and black pepper, and stir to mix well.

■ Reheat this sauce and serve it with grilled vegetables, or serve it with fish, over noodles, with chicken satay, etc.

nutritional analysis per serving
170.99 calories; 13.48 g fat (66% calories from fat);
3.87 g protein; 11.14 g carbohydrate; 0 mg cholesterol;
229.18 mg sodium

Strawberry Sauce

NO DAIRY, EGGS, OR NUTS

PREP TIME: 10 to 15 minutes ■ **SERVE:** Serves 8

I love this over a bowl of hot steel cut oats with a handful of chopped walnuts—it's a great way to start the day. This also tastes delicious served over yogurt, rice pudding, or cheese blintzes.

2 cups strawberries
¼ cup agave nectar
¼ cup water
2 tablespoons arrowroot
½ teaspoon ground cinnamon

■ Combine all ingredients in a saucepan and heat to boiling. Reduce the heat and continue cooking until the mixture thickens, about 10 minutes. Remove from heat. Serve over any dessert.

nutritional analysis per serving
40.11 calories; 0.12 g fat (2% calories from fat);
0.26 g protein; 11.42 g carbohydrate; 0 mg cholesterol;
0.59 mg sodium

Tofu Mayonnaise

NO DAIRY, EGGS, OR NUTS

PREP TIME: 10 minutes ■ **SERVE:** Makes 1½ cups

You may need to experiment with this recipe, adjusting the amounts of liquids to ensure the correct texture. Add the oil slowly and, if you prefer a thicker mayonnaise, use less water.

½ pound extra-firm tofu, drained
1 tablespoon lemon juice
1 teaspoon cider vinegar
½ teaspoon salt
¼ teaspoon Dijon mustard
¼ cup canola oil
1 tablespoon agave nectar

■ Slice the tofu into 1-inch slices and drain on paper towels for about 20 minutes, pressing out the moisture halfway through the draining process. Press again at the end of the 20 minutes. Place a few of the tofu slices in a blender with the lemon juice, cider vinegar, salt, and mustard. Mix until smooth, then add the rest of the tofu and the oil. When the mixture is well blended, add the agave nectar and stir.

■ Keep this mayo in the fridge. It will only last a week.

nutritional analysis per serving
41.83 calories; 3.81 g fat (80% of calories from fat);
1.32 g protein; 1.17 g carbohydrate; 0 mg cholesterol;
66.74 mg sodium

Tofu Pesto

PREP TIME: 10 minutes ■ **SERVE:** Serves 6

Tofu is a good source of protein, but it yields little flavor of its own. The basil and garlic really spice up this pesto. Be courageous and use it as a salad dressing or spread with vegetables in a lettuce wrap. I encourage you to be creative in the kitchen.

4 ounces firm tofu
2 tablespoons vegetable broth
2 cups fresh basil
2 cloves garlic
2 tablespoons lemon juice
3 tablespoons olive oil
½ cup fresh parsley
½ teaspoon ground pepper

■ Combine all ingredients in a blender and process until smooth.
■ Serve over rice noodles, polenta, or veggies.

nutritional analysis per serving
146.46 calories; 9.01 g fat (54% of calories from fat); 5.79 g protein; 16.75 g carbohydrate; 0.05 mg cholesterol; 47.23 mg sodium

Tofu Sour Cream

PREP TIME: 15 minutes ■ **SERVE:** Makes ½ cup

For those who are looking for an alternative to dairy, this sour cream recipe will fit the bill. You can also buy commercially prepared tofu sour cream in your local market if you don't have the time to whip this up.

1½ cups firm silken tofu
1 tablespoons lemon juice
1 tablespoon canola oil
1 teaspoon brown rice syrup
½ teaspoon salt
2 teaspoons cider vinegar
Water as needed

■ Put all ingredients in the blender and puree until smooth. If it is too thick, add a small amount of water to the mixture and blend.
■ Keep in the refrigerator. Will last up to 2 weeks.

nutritional analysis per serving
73.11 calories; 5.23 g fat (56% of calories from fat); 1.19 g protein; 6.51 g carbohydrate; 0 mg cholesterol; 199.94 mg sodium

Vegetarian Spaghetti Sauce

PREP TIME: 1½ to 2 hours
SERVE: Serves 6

This is one of my favorite sauces. It does lack protein, but you can add some tofu to the sauce and that will increase your protein. Fresh spinach in this sauce tastes great, too, and if you serve it over lentil pasta, you will balance your complex carbs with the protein.

1 large red onion, chopped
1 large red bell pepper, chopped
1 large zucchini, chopped
3 cloves garlic, minced
2 stalks celery, chopped
1 small eggplant, chopped
1 (14-ounce) can tomato sauce
1 (6-ounce) can tomato paste
8 ounces sun-dried tomatoes, chopped
½ cup vegetable broth
½ teaspoon freshly ground pepper
2 bay leaves
1 tablespoon fresh basil
2 teaspoons dried oregano

- Over medium heat, sauté all vegetables until soft, about 10 minutes. Add the tomato sauce, tomato paste, sun-dried tomatoes, vegetable broth, pepper, and herbs. Simmer for 1 hour. Remove bay leaves.
- Serve over rice or noodles.

> I prefer to cook this sauce longer so the flavors blend together well.

nutritional analysis per serving
75.36 calories; .85 g fat (10% of calories from fat); 2.73 g protein; 15.03 g carbohydrate; 0.21 mg cholesterol; 428.90 mg sodium

drinks

Chai Tea

PREP TIME: 15 minutes ■ **SERVE:** Serves 4

I recommend you double this recipe if you like chai tea as much as I do. If you prefer cow's milk to soy, you can easily substitute it. I wouldn't use rice milk though, as it changes the flavor too much.

½ teaspoon vanilla extract

4 cups soy milk

3 black tea bags

5 cinnamon sticks

1 teaspoon fennel seeds

6 cardamom pods

15 whole cloves

1 teaspoon ground coriander

grated nutmeg or ground cinnamon (optional)

agave nectar or brown rice syrup to sweeten (optional)

½-inch slice fresh ginger, grated

■ Combine the first seven ingredients in a saucepan and heat until the milk almost boils. Turn the heat to low and simmer for 10 to 15 minutes. Strain the mixture before serving. You can add grated nutmeg or cinnamon on top if you wish. You can also add a bit of agave or brown rice syrup, if you want it sweeter.

nutritional analysis per serving
180.07 calories; 5.98 g fat (272% calories from fat); 9.40 g protein; 29.97 g carbohydrate; 0 mg cholesterol; 38.41 mg sodium

Fancy Fruit Juice

PREP TIME: 5 minutes ■ **SERVE:** Serves 2

This is a quick, easy fruit juice that you can mix up by using different juices. Try grape and apple, or pineapple and mango juice, in place of the cran-raspberry juice.

1½ cups sparkling water

½ cup cran-raspberry juice, unsweetened

■ Combine juice and mineral water. Pour into ice-filled glasses and serve.

nutritional analysis per serving
34.30 calories; 0.06 g fat (1% calories from fat); 0.12 g protein; 8.57 g carbohydrate; 0 mg cholesterol; 3.62 mg sodium

Lemonade

PREP TIME: 5 minutes ■ **SERVE:** Serves 4

Who doesn't love fresh lemonade on a hot summer day? Feel free to adjust the amount of sweetener in this recipe. Why not toss in some fresh strawberries and whirl in the blender? Raspberries? Sounds heavenly.

¼ cup agave nectar

3½ cups water

½ cup lemon juice

■ Mix all ingredients together in a juice container and whisk together. Serve in iced glasses.

■ To make strawberry or raspberry lemonade, process the ingredients plus fresh berries in a blender for a special drink!

■ If agave nectar congeals, heat the water and stir well until blended, then cool.

nutritional analysis per serving
55.64 calories; 0 g fat (0% calories from fat); 0.12 g protein; 17.64 g carbohydrate; 0 mg cholesterol; 4.45 mg sodium

Smoothie

PREP TIME: 10 minutes ■ **SERVE:** Serves 4

To add more fiber to your diet, add 2 or 3 dried figs (ends removed) and 6 or 7 whole almonds. Bend until smooth. This smoothie is a quick breakfast drink or a midafternoon pick-me-up. It's also good before working out, or as an afterschool pick-me-up for the kids.

⅓ cup frozen orange juice concentrate

⅓ cup soy milk or rice milk

5 ice cubes

½ cup tofu

½ banana, mashed

¼ teaspoon vanilla extract

6 strawberries, blueberries. or raspberries, plus 4 extra berries, for garnish

2 tablespoons flaxseeds

■ Mix all ingredients in a blender and whirl until smooth. Serve with a frozen strawberry or raspberry on top.

> Note: Feel free to substitute fruit nectar for the orange juice, or to add yogurt, mango, or peaches.

nutritional analysis per serving
111.99 calories; 2.98 g fat (20% calories from fat); 3.47 g protein; 19.44 g carbohydrate; 0 mg cholesterol; 6.35 mg sodium

desserts

Almond Meal Piecrust

PREP TIME: 10 minutes to prepare, and than 30 minutes to bake
SERVE: Makes 2 piecrusts

I use this crust for pies that call for only a bottom crust. You can use it for a quiche crust, too, if you like. It has a nutty flavor and adds texture without a lot of carbohydrates.

2 cups almond meal
⅓ cup arrowroot
1 teaspoon baking powder
½ teaspoon xanthan gum
1 teaspoon salt
⅓ cup butter
⅓ cup water

- In a large bowl, combine the almond meal and arrowroot. Add the baking powder, xanthan gum, and salt, and mix well. Add the butter and mix with a fork/pastry cutter until the mixture is crumbly. Slowly add the water a little at a time, until the mixture forms a ball. Divide into 2 balls of equal size. Cover and chill. This dough tears easily, so use caution when rolling out. Roll out each ball between two sheets of waxed paper. Carefully transfer to a pie dish. If you are not adding a filling first, be sure to prick the bottom of the crust so it will not bubble up. Bake in a preheated 350°F oven for 30 minutes after you add the pie filling. Makes two crusts.

> For a nondairy alternative use buttery spread or organic shortening instead of butter.

nutritional analysis per serving
224.44 calories; 19.70 g fat (75% calories from fat); 5.15 g protein; 9.55 g carbohydrate; 20.34 mg cholesterol; 353.22 mg sodium

Almond Torte

NO DAIRY, EGGS, OR PEANUTS

PREP TIME: 30 minutes to prepare and about 1 hour to bake
SERVE: Serves 16

I was asked several years ago at a conference for health professionals to prepare a dessert that was not only sugar and gluten free, but also dairy and egg free. I tried several things before I came up with this dessert, and it was a huge hit. Be sure to serve it with the Berry Sauce on page 187. Can also be served with lemon curd. Hazelnuts work very well in place of the almonds, too.

½ cup oil

¾ cup agave nectar

1¼ cups unsweetened applesauce

1¼ cups soy milk

1½ cups unsweetened apple juice

1 teaspoon vanilla extract

1 teaspoon almond extract

4 cups brown rice flour

2 tablespoons baking powder

½ teaspoon salt

2 cups finely chopped or ground almonds

■ In a large bowl, mix together the oil and agave nectar until thick and creamy. Be sure the oil and sweetener are at room temperature to avoid curdling. Add the applesauce, soy milk, apple juice, vanilla, and almond extract.

■ Mix together the flour, baking powder, and salt in a large bowl. Add the almonds. Add the liquid ingredients to the dry ingredients and stir until they are blended. Do not over-mix.

■ Spray the bottoms of two 10-inch cake pans or one 9 × 13-inch rectangular pan with vegetable oil spray.

■ Preheat the oven to 350°F.

■ Pour the batter into the prepared pan(s) and bake for 45 to 55 minutes for the rounds, or 50 to 60 minutes for the rectangle, until the torte is lightly browned and a toothpick comes out clean when inserted into the middle of the cake.

■ Cool on a wire rack before you remove the torte from the pan(s). Do not cut into layers until completely cooled.

nutritional analysis per serving
373.90 calories; 16.92 g fat (39% calories from fat); 6.93 g protein; 52.26 g carbohydrate; 0 mg cholesterol; 204.0 mg sodium

Apple and Berry Crisp

PREP TIME: 15 minutes to prepare and 65 to 75 minutes to bake
SERVE: Serves 10

Another crowd-pleaser, this versatile recipe can be prepared as is, or with blueberries or other fruits. If your family doesn't care for nuts or has a nut allergy, replace the nuts with your favorite seeds or leave the nuts out— their omission won't change the consistency of the dish.

Fruit:

4 cups apples, peeled, cored, and sliced

5 cups strawberries, fresh or frozen, hulled

3 cups raspberries, fresh or frozen

½ teaspoon ground cinnamon

¼ teaspoon grated nutmeg

2 tablespoons arrowroot

1 tablespoon orange juice, fresh if possible

Topping:

6 tablespoons agave nectar

2 cups oats or rice flakes

½ cup brown rice flour

2 teaspoons ground cinnamon

½ teaspoon ground allspice

1 cup walnuts, chopped

½ cup buttery spread or non-dairy margarine

- Preheat oven to 350°F.
- In a large bowl, combine the fruit, cinnamon, nutmeg, and arrowroot. Squeeze the orange juice over the fruit and toss again. Place the fruit in a 9 × 13-inch pan that has been lightly sprayed with vegetable oil.
- Cover with foil and bake for about 45 minutes, until hot and the fruit is beginning to bubble.
- While the fruit is baking, mix together the agave nectar, oats, flour, cinnamon, allspice, and walnuts. Cut in the buttery spread until the mixture is crumbly.
- Remove the pan of fruit from the oven and spread the topping over the fruit. Return the pan to the oven and continue baking, uncovered, for another 20 to 30 minutes, or until the topping is browned.
- Serve hot or at room temperature. The crisp will thicken as it cools.

> You may substitute cornstarch for the arrowroot, if you prefer. Rice flakes can be used in place of the oats.

nutritional analysis per serving
332.51 calories; 18.11 g fat (48% calories from fat); 5.50 g protein; 42.28 g carbohydrate; 0 mg cholesterol; 99.07 mg sodium

Apple Cake

PREP TIME: 15 minutes to prepare and about 35 minutes to bake
SERVE: Serves 10

When you are looking for a cake to serve at a birthday party, or to use up apples in the fall, this is a great option.

½ cup agave nectar

⅓ cup plus 2 tablespoons shortening

¼ cup unsweetened applesauce

2 eggs

1 teaspoon vanilla extract

½ cup soy milk

1¾ cups brown rice flour

½ cup potato starch

1 tablespoon baking powder

1¼ teaspoon ground cinnamon

½ teaspoon salt

2 large apples

1 tablespoon brown rice syrup

■ Preheat the oven to 350°F. In a large mixing bowl, combine the agave nectar and ⅓ cup of the shortening. Beat well. Add the eggs and applesauce. and beat again. Add the vanilla and soy milk.

■ In a small bowl, sift the flour and potato starch together with the baking powder, 1 teaspoon of the cinnamon, and the salt. Add this mixture to the egg mixture and beat until smooth.

■ Grease an 8- to 9-inch springform pan with cooking oil and dust lightly with brown rice flour. Pour the batter into the pan. Peel, core, and slice the apples into equal-sized slices, and place them evenly around the perimeter of the cake.

■ In a small bowl, combine the remaining 2 tablespoons of shortening, the brown rice syrup, and the remaining ¼ teaspoon of cinnamon. Drizzle over the apples and bake for 30 to 35 minutes, or until a cake tester comes out clean.

nutritional analysis per serving
201.76 calories; 8.46 g fat (38% calories from fat);
6.5 g protein; 34 g carbohydrate; 3.83 mg cholesterol;
281.56 mg sodium

Apple Pie

PREP TIME: 10 minutes and 50 to 60 minutes to bake
SERVE: Serves 8

If you really want a delicious pie, and you don't mind the addition of dairy, dot a few pats of butter over the apples before adding the top crust. If you prefer to keep this dessert dairy free, it tastes just fine as it is.

5 cups apples, peeled, cored, and sliced

1 teaspoon ground cinnamon

2–3 tablespoons arrowroot

½–¾ cup agave or fruit sweetener

- Preheat the oven to 350°F.
- Toss all ingredients together and place in prepared piecrust (see page 223 for basic 2-crust piecrust). Bake for 50 to 60 minutes or until crust is browned.
- Variations: To add berries to the recipe, decrease the amount of apples to 4 cups and add 1 cup of either blueberries, strawberries, or raspberries.
- If you apples are really juicy, you will need the larger amount of arrowroot. If they are not too juicy, only use 2 tablespoons arrowroot. You can also adjust the sweetness to your liking, taking into account that ½ cup agave will be less sweet.

nutritional analysis per serving
134. calories; 0.25 g fat (2% calories from fat); 0.53 g protein; 38.0 g carbohydrate; 0 mg cholesterol; 1.14 mg sodium

Baked Apples

PREP TIME: 15 minutes to prepare and about 35 minutes to bake
SERVE: Serves 4

To make this dessert dairy free, instead of using the ricotta cheese, mash one block of firm tofu with a fork. Add a little lemon juice, salt, and nutmeg to taste. If you prefer it sweeter, add a small amount of agave nectar and stir to blend.

4 medium-size apples

4 tablespoons shortening

4 tablespoons walnuts, chopped

¾ teaspoon peeled and grated fresh ginger

4 cinnamon sticks

5 tablespoons fruit sweetener or agave nectar

Water as needed

¾ cup ricotta cheese (for a non-dairy cheese, see above note)

- Preheat the oven to 450°F. Wash the apples and level the bottoms by slicing off ¼-inch or so, to allow the apples to sit flat in the baking dish. Core them, and place them in a baking dish. Spoon 1 tablespoon of shortening, 1 tablespoon of chopped walnuts, a pinch of fresh ginger, and 1 cinnamon stick into each cored apple. Top with the fruit sweetener. Place a small amount of water in the bottom of the baking dish and bake in the oven for 30 to 35 minutes. Remove from the oven and cool slightly.
- Place the ricotta (or tofu if you wish it to be dairy-free—see note at left) in a blender and puree until smooth. Add 1 tablespoon of the sweetener and the remaining ginger. Blend until mixed and place 1 to 2 tablespoons on top of each baked apple. Serve warm.

> You may use other nuts in this recipe in place of the walnuts.

nutritional analysis per serving
363.15 calories; 20.63 g fat (49% calories from fat); 7.34 g protein; 47.11 g carbohydrate; 44.83 mg cholesterol; 63 mg sodium

Banana Bars

PREP TIME: 20 minutes to prepare and about 25 minutes to bake

SERVE: Serves 24 (1 bar per serving)

There are many gluten-free flours to choose from for this recipe. See section on flours (page 7). Betcha can't eat just one!

¾ cup shortening

⅔ cup fruit sweetener or agave nectar

2 eggs

1 teaspoon vanilla extract

2 medium-size ripe bananas, mashed

2 cups sorghum flour or rice flour

1 tablespoon baking powder

¼ teaspoon salt

½ teaspoon xanthan gum

½ cup pecans or walnuts, chopped

- Preheat the oven to 350°F. Be sure your sweetener and shortening are at room temperature. Cream together the shortening and fruit sweetener until thick. Add the egg and vanilla, and mix until blended. Stir in the mashed banana. In a small bowl, combine the flour, baking powder, xanthan gum, and salt. Add to the liquid mixture and beat until just combined. Add the pecans.
- Spoon evenly into a greased 9 × 11-inch baking pan.
- Bake for 25 minutes or until done. Cool and cut into 24 squares.

> These store well in an airtight container at room temperature, or can be frozen.

nutritional analysis per serving
141.67 calories; 6.10 g fat (39% calories from fat); 1.31 g protein; 21.70 g carbohydrate; 17.91 mg cholesterol; 114.69 mg sodium

Blackberry Cobbler

NO DAIRY OR NUTS

PREP TIME: 15 minutes to prepare and about 30 minutes to bake.
SERVE: Serves 8

Stoneyfield Farms makes a good-tasting soy yogurt. If you don't want to use soy yogurt, you can use nonfat yogurt and butter, but it will no longer be dairy free.

5 cups fresh blackberries, washed and drained

½ cup agave nectar or fruit sweetener

1 cup plus 2 tablespoons brown rice flour

1 teaspoon grated orange zest

2 tablespoons fresh orange juice

1½ teaspoons vanilla extract

½ cup soy yogurt

2 egg whites, beaten

2 tablespoons buttery spread, melted

1 cup brown rice flour

2 teaspoon baking powder

- Preheat the oven to 400°F.
- Combine the blackberries, agave, 2 tablespoons of the brown rice flour, orange peel, 1 of the orange juice, and 1 teaspoon of the vanilla. Mix well. Pour this mixture into a greased 9 × 11-inch pan.
- In a small bowl, combine the yogurt, ½ teaspoon vanilla, and egg whites. Beat together well. Add the melted buttery spread and the remaining tablespoon of orange juice. Mix well. Set aside.
- In a small bowl, combine the remaining 1 cup of brown rice flour with the baking powder. Mix well and add to the yogurt mixture. Stir together, but don't overmix. Dollop this mixture on top of the blackberry mixture and bake for 30 to 35 minutes, or until lightly browned and bubbly.

nutritional analysis per serving
189.51 calories; 3.44 g fat (16% calories from fat); 3.69 g protein; 39.33 g carbohydrate; 0.31 mg cholesterol; 70.97 mg sodium

Brown Rice Pudding

NO DAIRY, EGGS, OR NUTS

PREP TIME: 1 hour
SERVE: Serves 4

A delightful replacement for part or all of the milk in this recipe is coconut milk. It gives the rice pudding a smooth, creamy texture. Feel free to add mangoes or bananas, too. It's a great snack or good start to any day, served along with fresh fruits or juices.

3 cups soy milk (or rice milk, coconut milk or almond milk)

1 cup brown rice

3 tablespoons agave nectar or fruit sweetener (or brown rice syrup)

½ teaspoon vanilla extract

Dash of grated nutmeg

½ teaspoon ground cinnamon

■ Place the milk, rice, and agave nectar in a saucepan and bring to a boil. As soon as it begins to boil, reduce the heat to medium low and cover. Simmer for 50 to 60 minutes, or until the rice is cooked but not dry. Remove from the heat and add the vanilla, nutmeg and cinnamon.

> To prepare this for breakfast, add more protein, such as nuts or yogurt. I also add dates or raisins.

nutritional analysis per serving
281.93 calories; 4.52 g fat (14% calories from fat); 8.26 g protein; 58.25 g carbohydrate; 0 mg cholesterol; 97.58 mg sodium

Cashew Butter Cookies

NO DAIRY

PREP TIME: 10 minutes to prepare and about 30 minutes to bake
SERVE: Serves 18

Here's another good egg substitution that works well in cookies: Mix 3 tablespoons of water with 1 tablespoon of ground flaxseeds. Use in place of 1 egg. Using an egg substitute will reduce your cholesterol and calories.

1 cup shortening

¾ cup agave nectar or fruit sweetener

2 eggs or Ener-G egg substitute (see note)

1 teaspoon vanilla extract

1 cup cashew butter

1 cup garbanzo bean flour

1 cup crushed cornflakes

1 cup cashews or other nuts, chopped

¾ cup arrowroot

2 teaspoons baking soda

½ teaspoon xanthan gum

1 teaspoon salt

- Preheat the oven to 350°F.
- Combine the shortening and the agave nectar in a large mixing bowl. Be sure both ingredients are at room temperature to avoid curdling. Beat until creamed and fluffy. Add the cashew butter. Blend well. Add the eggs, one at a time, and then the vanilla. Beat well.
- Mix together in a small bowl the bean flour, cornflakes, almonds, arrowroot, baking soda, xanthan gum, and salt. Add to the liquid ingredients and mix until well blended. Drop by teaspoons onto ungreased cookie sheets.
- Bake 12 to 15 minutes. Makes 6 dozen 3-inch cookies.

nutritional analysis per serving
273.19 calories; 20.14 g fat (64% calories from fat); 4.48 g protein; 21.74 g carbohydrate; 27.26 mg cholesterol; 472.85 mg sodium

Chai Rice Pudding

PREP TIME: 50 minutes
SERVE: Serves 6

Here is another rice pudding that coconut milk really enhances. It stores well in the refrigerator and can be served warm or cold.

4 cups soy milk
1 cup arborio or long-grain rice
⅓ cup agave nectar
½ teaspoon ground ginger
¾ teaspoon ground cinnamon
½ teaspoon ground cardamom
½ teaspoon ground allspice

■ Combine soy milk, rice, and agave nectar in a saucepan. Bring to a boil and then reduce the heat and simmer, uncovered, for 45 to 50 minutes, or until the rice is tender. Stir occasionally and add the spices just before serving.

nutritional analysis per serving
173.46 calories; 3.37 g fat (12% calories from fat); 7.12 g protein; 36.02 g carbohydrate; 0 mg cholesterol; 99.20 mg sodium

Cheese Blintzes

PREP TIME: 10 minutes to prepare plus chilling time
SERVE: Serves 8

To make the best gluten-free, sugar-free dessert you have ever made, prepare the Crêpes found on page 214 and fill with this recipe. Serve with the Berry Sauce found on page 187 and you'll have a very hard time resisting these blintzes!

1 cup fresh ricotta cheese or cottage cheese
1 teaspoon vanilla extract
¼ cup agave nectar
½ cup cream cheese
1 recipe Crêpes

- To make the cheese filling, place the cottage cheese in a blender and puree until smooth. Add the rest of the ingredients and continue to puree until they are well mixed and smooth. Place the cheese filling in a bowl, cover, and refrigerate until ready to use. This mixture stores in the refrigerator for several days.
- Prepare crêpes as directed, and fill.

> The best gluten-free, sugar-free dessert.

nutritional analysis per serving
118.98 calories; 6.30 g fat (46% calories from fat); 6.32 g protein; 10.85 g carbohydrate; 17.08 mg cholesterol; 163.17 mg sodium

Chocolate Pudding

PREP TIME: 5 minutes to prepare and 1 to 2 hours to chill
SERVE: Serves 4

Your kids will love this recipe. It's easy to make and you won't feel guilty about eating it, as it is quite good for you.

2 (12-ounce) packages firm silken tofu

2 teaspoons vanilla extract

¾ cup agave nectar

½ cup cocoa powder

- Place the tofu in a blender and puree until smooth. Add the vanilla. Blend.
- In a separate bowl, combine the agave nectar and the cocoa powder. Stir to mix well. Add to the tofu mixture and blend until well mixed. Pour into serving dishes and refrigerate for a few hours.

nutritional analysis per serving
197.82 calories; 2.61 g fat (6% of calories from fat); 4.12 g protein; 52.34 g carbohydrate; 0 mg cholesterol; 4.55 mg sodium

Coconut Sorbet

NO DAIRY, EGGS, OR NUTS

PREP TIME: 10 minutes to prepare; follow manufacturer's recommendations for freezing times

SERVE: Serves 6

If you like coconut, you'll love this sorbet. You must have an ice cream or frozen yogurt machine to make it. It is wonderful with grated fresh ginger as a garnish. This can be made a day ahead if needed.

2 cups water

1 cup coconut milk

2 tablespoons agave nectar or fruit sweetener

¼ cup toasted coconut or peeled and grated fresh ginger

- In a large bowl, combine all the ingredients except the toasted coconut. Mix well and place in the refrigerator to chill.
- To make the sorbet, use an ice-cream machine. Follow the instructions for making sorbet as provided by the manufacturer.

nutritional analysis per serving
314.68 calories; 19.72 g fat (52% of calories from fat); 2.01 g protein; 36.69 g carbohydrate; 0 mg cholesterol; 175.95 mg sodium

Crêpes

NO DAIRY OR NUTS

PREP TIME: About 30 minutes
SERVE: Serves 6 (2 crêpes apiece)

Nobody will ever know these crêpes are made without wheat flour. These crêpes are very versatile—they can be used for the Cheese Blintzes found on page 211, or they can be used as dinner crêpes, filled with the Black Bean Burrito mixture found on page 135, or as a dessert filling with fresh fruit. Make and store them in the refrigerator between waxed paper in an airtight container for future use.

2 large eggs
¾ cup soy milk
6 tablespoons arrowroot
1 tablespoon canola oil
1 teaspoon baking powder
¼ teaspoon salt
Vegetable oil spray

- In a large bowl, beat the eggs until fluffy. Add the soy milk, arrowroot, oil, baking powder, and salt. Beat until well blended.
- Spray an 8-inch skillet with vegetable oil spray and place over medium-low heat. Add about 2 tablespoons of the milk mixture to the skillet and tilt the pan so the mixture spreads evenly over the entire surface. You must spread the mixture quickly because these cook fast. When the crêpe is lightly browned, carefully turn it over. Be careful not to overcook the crêpe, which will cause it to stick to the skillet. Transfer to a plate and cool. Repeat with remaining batter. Makes about 12 crêpes (if you want thicker crêpes, add more mixture to the skillet and you will end up with about 8 crêpes instead of 12). When cool, place each crêpe between waxed paper or serve immediately.

nutritional analysis per serving
90.41 calories; 4.71 g fat (46% of calories from fat); 3.13 g protein; 8.82 g carbohydrate; 72.94 mg cholesterol; 215.99 mg sodium

Granola Piecrust

NO DAIRY OR EGGS

PREP TIME: 10 minutes to prepare and 15 to 20 minutes to bake
SERVE: Makes 1 crust

This piecrust can only be used for an open-top pie. It works well for Tofu Cheesecake (page 231) as it adds a great nutty taste. It would be great for a pumpkin pie or apple torte as well.

1¼ cup oats

½ cup oat flour or brown rice flour

1 cup chopped nuts (I favor walnuts)

¼ cup sesame seeds

3 tablespoons sunflower or pumpkin seeds, chopped

1 teaspoon ground cinnamon

7 tablespoons shortening

¼ cup agave nectar, fruit sweetener, or brown rice syrup

- In a large bowl, stir together the oats, oat flour, chopped nuts, sesame seeds, sunflower seeds, and cinnamon. Cut in the shortening a little at a time until the mixture resembles coarse peas. Drizzle the agave nectar on top, and stir well to combine. The mixture needs to be well mixed to hold together well in the pie shell.
- Press this mixture into a greased pie shell and bake in a preheated 350°F oven for 15 to 20 minutes, or fill with your favorite pie filling and bake according to the directions.

nutritional analysis per serving
396.31 calories; 23.67 g fat (51% calories from fat); 5.78 g protein; 42.32 g carbohydrate; 6.27 mg cholesterol; 40.55 mg sodium

Healthy Candy

PREP TIME: 20 minutes
SERVE: Serves 10 (2 pieces each serving)

If nuts are a problem for you, try sesame butter or pumpkin seed butter, and use seeds in place of the nuts. There is no set rule on this recipe. Replace the currants with dates or dried cranberries, or live large and add carob chips.

1 cup brown rice syrup
1 cup almond butter
¼ teaspoon vanilla extract
¼ cup chopped walnuts
2 tablespoons flaxseeds
3 tablespoons currants

- Heat the brown rice syrup and almond butter in a medium-size saucepan, making sure to stir the mixture constantly, as otherwise it will burn. Bring to a boil, then reduce heat to low and continue to cook for another 5 minutes. Be sure to continue stirring to avoid burning.
- Remove from heat and add the remaining ingredients.
- Mix until well blended. Drop onto parchment paper and refrigerate.

nutritional analysis per serving
207.83 calories; 17.51 g fat (70% calories from fat); 4.89 g protein; 11.63 g carbohydrate; 0 mg cholesterol; 116.59 mg sodium

The Ladies' Favorite Meringue

PREP/COOK TIME: 30 to 40 minutes
SERVE: Serves 10

This recipe received its name because all of my lady friends loved it. They argued over who got to take home the leftovers when I made it for one of my "taster's parties." It serves many, so it is great for a potluck or large gathering when a light, low calorie dessert is preferred.

3 cups frozen strawberries, thawed and sliced

2 cups frozen blueberries, thawed

¼ cup orange juice

1 teaspoon vanilla extract

1 tablespoon arrowroot

6 egg whites

- Preheat the oven to 375°F.
- Place the strawberries, blueberries, orange juice, and vanilla in a saucepan. Stir well and bring to a boil. Add the arrowroot to the mixture slowly, whisking constantly until dissolved. Reduce the heat and simmer until the mixture begins to thicken, 3 to 4 minutes. Stir often so the mixture does not burn. Once the mixture has thickened and has a shiny surface, remove from the heat and pour into a bowl to cool.
- Meanwhile, beat the egg whites until they are stiff. Fold gently into the cooled berry mixture.
- Pour into a 9 × 13-inch baking dish and place it in a larger pan. Fill that pan with hot water until it is about halfway up the sides. Carefully place in the oven and bake for 20 minutes. Watch the baking time, as oven heat varies. Remove the baking dish from the pan with water and return it to the oven for another 3 minutes. The meringue should be lightly browned.
- Let cool for 20 to 30 minutes before serving. May be served warm or cold.

nutritional analysis per serving
49.22 calories; 0.28 g fat (5% of calories of fat);
2.72 g protein; 9.49 g carbohydrate; 0 mg cholesterol;
34.27 mg sodium

Lavender and Berry Crisp

NO EGGS

PREP TIME: 1¼ hours
SERVE: Serves 8

I love lavender and grow it in my garden so I have it available all year to use in my recipes. I like having some of the lavender buds in crisp, but you don't have to use them. If you sift the buds, only the essence will come through. Lavender pairs very well with lemon, pears, and peaches, too, so feel free to use other fruits in this recipe.

1 tablespoon Provence culinary-grade lavender buds

¾ cup agave nectar

4 cups blueberries

4 cups raspberries or any other berry

1 tablespoon orange or lemon juice

1 teaspoon ground cinnamon

2 tablespoons arrowroot

¼ cup butter or shortening

½ cup oats or rice flakes

1 cup brown rice flour

¾ cup walnuts, chopped

- Preheat the oven to 350°F.
- Sift or grind the lavender buds and place in a large mixing bowl. (I throw many of the buds into the bowl whole, but you can also grind all the buds if you prefer). Add the agave nectar, berries, juice, cinnamon, and arrowroot. Stir together well and pour this mixture into a greased 9-inch square baking dish. Set aside.
- In a small bowl, combine the butter, oats, and brown rice flour. Cut with a fork or pastry cutter until the mixture resembles small peas. Add the walnuts and mix together. Sprinkle this mixture over the berries and bake for 1 hour. Cool completely before serving.

nutritional analysis per serving
340.89 calories; 8.84 g fat (20% calories from fat); 3.14 g protein; 67.46 g carbohydrate; 30.50 mg cholesterol; 4.14 mg sodium

Mango Mousse

PREP TIME: 65 minutes to prepare and 60 minutes to chill
SERVE: Serves 4

I like this dessert best in summer, but if you have access to fresh mangoes any time of year, it is a great light and fluffy dessert. Serve it following an Indian or Asian meal, or simply by itself.

2 ripe mangoes, pitted, peeled
Water (to add to mango mixture)
1 tablespoon arrowroot
1 tablespoon agave nectar
1 tablespoon fresh orange juice
   or lemon juice
2 cups fresh whipped cream

- Place the mangoes in a blender and puree. Once the mixture is blended, add enough water to create 2 cups of puree. Pour into a saucepan and bring to a boil over a medium-high heat.
- In a small bowl combine the arrowroot and agave nectar. Stir until well blended. Add to the mango mixture and stir until mixed. Add the orange juice and place in a large bowl. Place this mixture in the freezer for about 1 hour.
- Remove from the freezer and beat with a mixer for 2 to 3 minutes, or until the mixture becomes thick and creamy.
- In a small bowl whip the cream until light and fluffy. Fold into the mango mixture and transfer to individual serving dishes. Cover with plastic wrap and refrigerate until set.

> You can substitute peaches or other fruits or berries for the mangoes.

nutritional analysis per serving
153.35 calories; 6.91 g fat (40% calories from fat); 1.44 g protein; 24.09 g carbohydrate; 22.80 mg cholesterol; 40.77 mg sodium

Marionberry Bars

PREP TIME: 10 minutes to prepare and 35 to 45 to bake
SERVE: Serves 12

Have no fear. *If you don't have Marion-berry jam at your local market, this recipe is very versatile and can be made with any sugar-free jam. My favorite is Marionberry, but after that, I love raspberry, strawberry, and blueberry. They all taste great in this recipe.*

½ cup agave nectar or fruit sweetener, at room temperature

1 cup shortening, at room temperature

1 large egg, lightly beaten

2⅛ cups brown rice flour or sorghum

1 cup walnuts or pecans, chopped finely

vegetable oil spray

1 (10-ounce) jar all-fruit jam (Marionberry, if possible)

- Preheat the oven to 350°F.
- Combine the agave nectar and shortening in a large mixing bowl and beat until light and fluffy. Be sure the agave and shortening are both at room temperature to avoid curdling.
- Add the egg, flour, and nuts. Beat at low speed until well mixed. Set aside 1 to 1½ cups of the mixture to use for the topping. Press the remaining mixture into the bottom of an 8-inch square pan that has been sprayed lightly with vegetable oil spray. Spread the jam on top to within half an inch of the edge. Dollop the reserved mixture over the top.
- Bake for 35 to 45 minutes or until browned. Do not over-bake. Cool and cut into bars.

> The buttery spread used in this recipe is a vegan spread and contains no saturated fats.

nutritional analysis per serving
380.53 calories; 22.58 g fat (51% calories from fat); 3.92 g protein; 44.36 g carbohydrate; 61.12 mg cholesterol; 9.04 mg sodium

Oat Scones

PREP/COOK TIME: 30 minutes
SERVE: 8 (makes 16, 2 scones per serving)

I made these oat scones for my cooking class, and they really enjoyed them. I served them warm with butter, but you can replace the butter with a soy margarine or just serve with an all-fruit jam. They keep for about a week if stored in an airtight container.

⅓ cup oil

2 tablespoons agave nectar

2 tablespoons warm water

1 tablespoon lemon juice (optional)

½ cup oat flour (or more as needed)

½ teaspoon baking soda

⅓ cup currants or raisins

⅓ cup rolled oats

- Preheat the oven to 325°F.
- In a 3-quart saucepan, combine the oil, agave nectar, water, and lemon juice, and heat until the agave nectar is combined with the oil and water. Remove from heat.
- In a small bowl, mix together the oat flour and baking soda. Stir into the oil mixture. Add the currants. Beat with a wooden spoon until mixed well.
- Add additional oat flour until you can form a ball. The dough should not be real sticky. Split the dough into two equal parts.
- Place about ¼ cup of rolled oats on the board where you are working. Roll one of the balls upon the oats and then press it flat until it becomes a 5-inch circle about ½ inch thick. Place on an ungreased cookie sheet that has been lightly covered with rolled oats. Do the same for the other ball. Bake for 20 to 25 minutes, or until lightly browned.
- Cool on a wire rack and serve.

nutritional analysis
125.884 calories; 9.20 g fat (64% calories from fat); 1.23 g protein; 10.51 g carbohydrate; 0 mg cholesterol; 155 mg sodium

Pear Torte

PREP TIME: 10 to 15 minutes to prepare and 30 minutes to bake
SERVE: Serves 12

I teach cooking classes, and this recipe is by far the favorite with my students. Double the recipe for parties; I guarantee it'll be a big hit. Organic pears are the best, but use canned when fresh are out of season. Don't overbake this torte; it should be set but not browned on top.

½ cup buttery spread or butter

⅓ cup + ⅛ cup agave nectar or fruit sweetener

¼ teaspoon vanilla extract

¾ cup brown rice flour

⅔ cup pecans or walnuts, chopped finely

8 ounces cream cheese, softened

1 egg

½ teaspoon vanilla extract

1 pound pears, fresh if possible, peeled, seeded, and sliced

Ground cinnamon, for sprinkling

- Preheat the oven to 350°F.
- To prepare the crust, mix together the buttery spread and ⅓ cup of the agave nectar. Be sure both ingredients are at room temperature. Blend until light and fluffy. Add the vanilla, flour, and nuts. Press these ingredients into the bottom of a 9-inch square pan and bake for 10 minutes, or until set. Let cool for a few minutes.
- For the filling: Mix the cream cheese and remaining ⅛ cup of the agave nectar until thoroughly mixed and fluffy. Add the egg and vanilla. Beat until smooth. Pour over the crust. Arrange the fresh pear slices on top of the filling. (If using canned pears, drain thoroughly and arrange on top of the filling.)
- Sprinkle lots of cinnamon on top and bake for 30 minutes at 350°F. If your oven tends to be hot, reduce the heat to 325°F. When you test for doneness, the filling should be set but not browned.

nutritional analysis per serving
259.77 calories; 19.10 g fat (65% calories from fat); 3.28 g protein; 21.24 g carbohydrate; 41.71 mg cholesterol; 144.22 mg sodium

Piecrust

PREP TIME: 15 minutes
SERVE: Serves 8

This is a great piecrust recipe, but it takes patience and practice to make. Roll out carefully as it is a bit fragile (no gluten to hold it together). It is certainly worth the effort.

1½ cups brown rice flour
½ cup potato starch flour
½ teaspoon salt
1 teaspoon xanthan gum
¼ cup arrowroot
¾ cup shortening
1 large egg, beaten
2 tablespoons water
1 tablespoon white vinegar

- In a large bowl, sift together the flour, potato starch, salt, and arrowroot. Add the xanthan gum. Stir to mix. Cut in the shortening with a pastry cutter until the mixture resembles small peas. Set aside.
- In a separate bowl, combine the egg, water, and vinegar, and add to the flour mixture. Mix until well blended and the mixture comes together in a large ball.
- Place a piece of waxed paper on a flat surface and cut the large ball into two smaller ones. Place one ball on the waxed paper and cover it with another piece of waxed paper of the same size. Carefully roll out the dough.
- Grease a pie dish and carefully flip the pie dough from the waxed paper into the dish. Fill with the pie ingredients. Roll out the second ball of dough, place atop the filling, and crimp the edges to seal.
- Cut slits in the crust before baking, and watch to be sure the crust does not brown too much around the edges while baking. If it does, cover with aluminum foil for the remainder of the baking time.
- Bake in a preheated 375°F oven or follow the directions for baking temperature for your desired filling.

nutritional analysis per serving
206.60 calories; 17.32 g fat (76% calories from fat); 0.80 g protein; 11.64 g carbohydrate; 26.44 mg cholesterol; 190.01 mg sodium

Pumpkin Bars

PREP/COOK TIME: 40–45 minutes
SERVE: 24

These pumpkin bars are great for the kids to take to school, or to have as an afternoon snack. Heck, forget about the kids; they are great for adults, too! I have people tell me all the time they don't believe these are sugar and gluten free.

2 cups sorghum flour

2 teaspoons baking powder

2 teaspoons ground cinnamon

1 teaspoon baking soda

¼ teaspoon salt

4 eggs

1 (14-ounce) can pureed pumpkin

¾ cup agave nectar

¾ cup unsweetened applesauce

¼ cup canola oil

¾ cup chopped walnuts or pecans (optional)

- Preheat the oven to 350°F.
- In a medium-size bowl, stir together the flour, baking powder, cinnamon, salt, and baking soda. In a large bowl, beat together the agave nectar and oil until smooth. Add the eggs, pumpkin, and applesauce. Add the flour mixture to the liquid ingredients. Beat until combined. Stir in the nuts.
- Spread the batter in an ungreased 9 × 11 baking pan. Bake for 25 to 35 minutes, or until a toothpick comes out clean. Cool on a wire rack. Cut into 24 squares.

nutritional analysis
149.41.74 calories; 6.00 g fat (35.5% calories from fat); 2.93 g protein; 21.65 g carbohydrate; 35.25 mg cholesterol; 12.72 mg sodium

Pumpkin Tofu Cookies

PREP TIME: 10 minutes to prepare and 30 to 45 minutes to bake
SERVE: Serves 12

These cookies must be stored in the refrigerator. They are great for anyone with food allergies, as there are no nuts, eggs, or dairy, nor gluten or sugar. I think you will be pleasantly surprised at how good these taste.

1 tablespoons ground flaxseeds

3 tablespoons water

⅓ cup canola oil

½ cup agave nectar

1 teaspoon vanilla extract

2 tablespoons extra-firm tofu, mashed

1 cup canned pureed pumpkin

1½ cups garbanzo bean flour

1 teaspoon baking powder

½ teaspoon baking soda

½ teaspoon grated nutmeg

1 teaspoon ground cinnamon

½ teaspoon salt

½ cup pumpkin seeds, chopped

½ cup chopped dates or raisins

- Preheat the oven to 375°F.
- In a coffee grinder or blender, grind the flaxseeds and mix with the water. Set aside. You will use this to replace egg in this recipe. In a mixing bowl, combine the oil and agave nectar. Mix until well blended and smooth. Add the flaxseed mixture, vanilla, tofu, and pumpkin. Mix together well. In a medium-size bowl, combine the flour, baking powder, baking soda, nutmeg, cinnamon, and salt. Stir together and slowly add this mixture to the pumpkin mixture, stirring to mix well. Add the pumpkin seeds and chopped dates.
- Drop by tablespoons onto a baking sheet. Flatten slightly and bake at 375°F for 12 to 15 minutes. Be sure to check on the cookies, as heat varies from oven to oven. Cool on wire racks. Makes 3 dozen.

nutritional analysis per serving
149.72 calories; 8.03 g fat (47% calories from fat);
2.84 g protein; 20.09 g carbohydrate; 0 mg cholesterol;
159.91 mg sodium

Raspberry Mousse

NO DAIRY, EGGS, OR NUTS

PREP TIME: 10 minutes to prepare and 1 hour to chill

SERVE: Serves 4

I love desserts that take little effort and have few calories. This mousse is light and easy to make. If you don't eat it all in one evening, cover and store in the refrigerator.

½ pound extra-firm tofu

1 cup raspberries

3 tablespoons frozen orange juice concentrate

2 tablespoons frozen pineapple or apple juice concentrate

1 tablespoon arrowroot

- Place the tofu in a blender and puree until smooth. Add the raspberries, orange juice, pineapple juice, and arrowroot. Blend until smooth. You can add more juice or less depending on how you like it.
- Spoon into serving dishes. Keep refrigerated until served.

nutritional analysis per serving
66.70 calories; 0.96 g fat (12% calories from fat);
2.05 g protein; 13.50 g carbohydrate; 0 mg cholesterol;
2.45 mg sodium

Roasted Pears

PREP/COOK TIME: 25 minutes
SERVE: Serves 4

This is a very *light, refreshing dessert that can also be made with other fruits, such as peaches, nectarines, or apples. It's easy to make and offers few calories.*

3 large pears, cored, peeled, and quartered
¼ cup agave nectar
½ teaspoon ground cinnamon
¼ teaspoon ground cardamom
¼ teaspoon grated nutmeg

- Preheat the oven to 350°F.
- Place the pears in an 8-inch square baking dish. In a small bowl, combine the agave nectar, cinnamon, cardamom, and nutmeg, then pour over the pears. Cover and bake for 25 minutes. Check at 20 minutes; if they are tender and bubbly, they are done! Baste with the juices.

nutritional analysis per serving
80.20 calories; 0.18 g fat (2% of calories from fat);
0.50 g protein; 21.26 g carbohydrate; 0 mg cholesterol;
1.80 mg sodium

Sesame Candy

PREP TIME: 10 minutes to prepare and 1 hour to chill
SERVE: Serves 10

This candy can be made nut free by simply replacing the almond butter with sesame butter. It is gooey, and the kids will love it. It tends to stick to the parchment paper, so you may want to spray the parchment with oil lightly before dropping the candy onto the cookie sheet.

¼ cup brown rice syrup
½ cup almond butter
1 cup sesame seeds
¼ cup arrowroot or quinoa flour

■ Mix all ingredients together in a large bowl. Drop by spoonfuls onto a cookie sheet lined with parchment paper and place in the refrigerator. Makes 20 pieces.

nutritional analysis per serving
175.81 calories; 14.54 g fat (69% calories from fat); 4.47 g protein; 9.63 g carbohydrate; 0 mg cholesterol; 58.65 mg sodium

Strawberry Shortcake

PREP TIME: 10 minutes to prepare and 15 minutes to bake
SERVE: Serves 6

This is "strawberry" shortcake, but you can use this shortcake for any fresh fruit. It stores well in the refrigerator.

3 large eggs

5 tablespoons nonfat yogurt or soy yogurt

1 tablespoon brown rice syrup

¾ cup brown rice flour

⅔ cup sorghum flour

1 tablespoon baking powder

¼ cup butter or non-dairy buttery spread

- Preheat the oven to 400°F.
- In a medium-size bowl, beat the eggs and add the yogurt and brown rice syrup. Stir until well blended. Set aside.
- In a large bowl, sift the flours and baking powder together. Cut in the butter until it resembles small peas. Add the yogurt mixture to the dry ingredients and stir until well blended.
- Press into a pie dish or a square baking pan and bake at 400°F for 15 minutes, or until lightly browned around the edges. Do not overbake.
- Serve with fresh strawberries and a nondairy topping or whipped cream.

nutritional analysis per serving
147.86 calories; 10.06 g fat (61% calories from fat); 4.38 g protein; 13.55 g carbohydrate; 106.01 mg cholesterol; 470.72 mg sodium

Strawberry Sorbet

PREP TIME: 10 minutes
SERVE: Serves 4

This dessert doesn't go into the freezer or ice-cream maker before serving. You simply place all of the frozen ingredients together in a blender and whirl. It's also good with a banana or, for some extra protein, add some tofu. The kids will never know it's good for them.

2 cups frozen strawberries
1 cup frozen blueberries
½ cup frozen orange juice

- Place all of the ingredients in a blender and process until smooth. If the mixture is too dry, add more orange juice concentrate.
- You can also use frozen pineapple juice, mango juice, etc. Be creative! Serve with whipped topping or fresh mint.

nutritional analysis per serving
101.43 calories; 0.42 g fat (3% calories from fat);
1.63 g protein; 24.64 g carbohydrate; 0 mg cholesterol;
2.19 mg sodium

Tofu Cheesecake

PREP TIME: 10 minutes to prepare and 50 to 60 minutes to bake
SERVE: Serves 8

You may be surprised to find that there's no hint of tofu when you taste this cheesecake. Tofu tends to absorb the flavors around it, and the lime, bananas, and pineapple mask its existence quite well. Enjoy.

1 Granola Piecrust (see page 215)

2 large eggs

½ cup agave nectar or fruit sweetener

2 tablespoons lime juice

1 teaspoon lime peel

1 teaspoon vanilla extract

2 medium-size bananas

1 pound firm tofu

8 ounces crushed unsweetened pineapple, drained

Seasonal fruits or berries

- Preheat the oven to 350°F.
- Prepare the granola piecrust and bake it for 15 minutes. Let cool.
- In a blender, combine the eggs and agave nectar and blend until well mixed. Add the lime juice, peel, and vanilla. Blend to mix. Break off chunks of the bananas and add to the mixture, mixing well. Add chunks of the tofu and continue to blend. Keep adding the tofu and bananas alternately until the mixture is smooth and well mixed.
- Pour into a large bowl and add the pineapple. Pour into the cooled pie shell. Lower the oven temperature to 325°F and bake for 50 to 60 minutes, or until the center of the cheesecake is set.
- Cool on a wire rack. Keep in the refrigerator.
- Top with fresh strawberries, blueberries, or whatever is in season.

nutritional analysis per serving
182.58 calories; 4.98 g fat (23% of calories of fat); 8.23 g protein; 31.86 g carbohydrate; 52.88 mg cholesterol; 24.11 mg sodium

Tofu Pumpkin Pie

NO DAIRY, EGGS, OR NUTS

PREP TIME: 10 minutes to prepare and 60 minutes to bake
SERVE: Serves 8

I worked for a very long time to come up with a dairy-free, egg-free pumpkin pie. You can also use either the Granola Piecrust (215) or the Almond Meal Piecrust (page 200) for this pie.

1 (9-inch) pie crust
1 pound extra-firm tofu
⅔–1 cup agave nectar
3 cups pureed pumpkin
2 tablespoons molasses
2 teaspoons ground cinnamon
1½ teaspoons ground ginger
1 teaspoon grated nutmeg
½ teaspoon ground allspice
1 tablespoon vanilla extract
3 tablespoons brown rice flour
2 teaspoons sesame tahini

- Preheat the oven to 400°F.
- Prepare the piecrust but do not bake.
- Drain the tofu on paper towels, then process in a blender until smooth. Add the rest of the ingredients and continue to blend until all of the ingredients are mixed together. Scrape the sides of the blender often and make sure the mixture is smooth before adding to the pie shell.
- Pour into a piecrust and bake at 400°F for about 1 hour, or until the center is set. Cool on a wire rack.

nutritional analysis per serving
232.33 calories; 4.95 g fat (18% of calories from fat);
7.18 g protein; 45.13 g carbohydrate; 0 mg cholesterol;
231.73 mg sodium

METRIC CONVERSIONS

› The recipes in this book have not been tested with metric measurements, so some variations might occu
› Remember that the weight of dry ingredients varies according to the volume or density factor: 1 cup of flour weighs far less than 1 cup of sugar, and 1 tablespoon doesn't necessarily hold 3 teaspoons.

— General Formulas for Metric Conversion

Ounces to grams	⇒ ounces × 28.35 = grams
Grams to ounces	⇒ grams × 0.035 = ounces
Pounds to grams	⇒ pounds × 453.5 = grams
Pounds to kilograms	⇒ pounds × 0.45 = kilograms
Cups to liters	⇒ cups × 0.24 = liters
Fahrenheit to Celsius	⇒ (°F − 32) × 5 ÷ 9 = °C
Celsius to Fahrenheit	⇒ (°C × 9) ÷ 5 + 32 = °F

— Linear Measurements

½ inch = 1½ cm
1 inch = 2½ cm
6 inches = 15 cm
8 inches = 20 cm
10 inches = 25 cm
12 inches = 30 cm
20 inches = 50 cm

— Volume (Dry) Measurements

¼ teaspoon = 1 milliliter
½ teaspoon = 2 milliliters
¾ teaspoon = 4 milliliters
1 teaspoon = 5 milliliters
1 tablespoon = 15 milliliters
¼ cup = 59 milliliters
⅓ cup = 79 milliliters
½ cup = 118 milliliters
⅔ cup = 158 milliliters
¾ cup = 177 milliliters
1 cup = 225 milliliters
4 cups or 1 quart = 1 liter
½ gallon = 2 liters
1 gallon = 4 liters

— Volume (Liquid) Measurements

1 teaspoon = ⅙ fluid ounce = 5 milliliters
1 tablespoon = ½ fluid ounce = 15 milliliters
2 tablespoons = 1 fluid ounce = 30 milliliters
¼ cup = 2 fluid ounces = 60 milliliters
⅓ cup = 2⅔ fluid ounces = 79 milliliters
½ cup = 4 fluid ounces = 118 milliliters
1 cup or ½ pint = 8 fluid ounces = 250 milliliters
2 cups or 1 pint = 16 fluid ounces = 500 milliliters
4 cups or 1 quart = 32 fluid ounces = 1,000 milliliters
1 gallon = 4 liters

— Oven Temperature Equivalents, Fahrenheit (F) and Celsius (C)

100°F = 38°C
200°F = 95°C
250°F = 120°C
300°F = 150°C
350°F = 180°C
400°F = 205°C
450°F = 230°C

— Weight (Mass) Measurements

1 ounce = 30 grams
2 ounces = 55 grams
3 ounces = 85 grams
4 ounces = ¼ pound = 125 grams
8 ounces = ½ pound = 240 grams
12 ounces = ¾ pound = 375 grams
16 ounces = 1 pound = 454 grams

Acknowledgments

I WOULD LIKE to thank the following people for their support. Carol Dudley, my oldest and dearest friend, who is a beacon of light and love in my life. My agent, Judy Hansen, the folks at Marlowe & Company, Mike Burkhart, Stephanie Ann, Marcia Doran, Barb Schiltz, Sheila Quinn, Dara Morgan, Connie Harrington, Bruce and the gang at Wholefoods Market in Gig Harbor, Daniel Roso, who tasted every recipe and provided excellent suggestions, the taste testers at the Functional Medicine Research Center, my CME colleagues Margaret Dicolli, Steve Passin, and Judy Sweetnam. A special thanks to all of my family, especially my brother Terry. Lastly, and most importantly, a very heartfelt thank you to my sons, Jeff and Rory, for your unending love and support.

Index